BREAKING THROUGH

WALTER and DOROTHY SCHWARZ

Breaking Through

Theory and Practice of Wholistic Living

GREEN BOOKS

First published by
Green Books
Hartland
Bideford
Devon, EX39 6EE

Cover: Simon Willby

British Library Cataloguing in Publication Data
Schwarz, Walter
Breaking Through: theory and practice of wholistic living
1. Human ecology
I. Title II. Schwarz. Dorothy
304' .2   GF41

Typeset by KMA Typesetting
70 The Square, Hartland, Devon

Printed by Robert Hartnoll (1985) Ltd.
Victoria Square, Bodmin, Cornwall

Contents

Preface

Introduction

CHAPTER ONE · A World View 3

CHAPTER TWO · Breaking Through 19

CHAPTER THREE · New Economics 33

CHAPTER FOUR · Ownwork 55

CHAPTER FIVE · Decolonised Communities 71

CHAPTER SIX · Sustainable Development 89

CHAPTER SEVEN · Appropriate Technology 109

CHAPTER EIGHT · Deep Ecology 125

CHAPTER NINE · Sustainable Agriculture 149

CHAPTER TEN · Sustainable Health 171

CHAPTER ELEVEN · The Feminine Principle 189

CHAPTER TWELVE · Human Scale Education 213

CHAPTER THIRTEEN · The Spiritual Dimension 235

CHAPTER FOURTEEN · Green Future 253

Conclusion

Bibliography

Index

Grateful acknowledgement is made for permission to reprint:

Excerpts from: *New Ideas in Ecology and Economics*, Copyright 1980 David Cayley, first aired by the Canadian Broadcasting Cooperation 1986.

Selected brief quotations and quiz (pp. 22-23) from: Bill Devall and George Sessions, *Deep Ecology*, Gibbs M. Smith Inc., 1983, Salt Lake City.

Selected quotations from: Donald Worster, *Nature's Economy*, Cambridge University Press.

Selected quotations from: E. Fromm, *To Have or To Be*, Jonathan Cape Ltd.

Permission was sought to reprint excerpts from: E. Fromm, *The Anatomy of Human Destructiveness*, CBS College Publishing, NY.

Photographs by permission of the Guardian, Rosemary and Penelope Ellis, and Tony Gibson (Lightfoot Project).

The picture on the cover courtesy of Die Grunen, West Germany.

Preface

TIME MAY telescope the memory but compression provides emphasis, enhancing the priorities of the mind. Perhaps these are the windows that Blake saw as chinks in the darkness, carrying the fragile tentacles of perception into four dimensions, steadying our grasp of ourselves and the world. I recall bumping along gently in an airport bus outside Geneva, probably in the late 60s, talking to Fritz Schumacher about an international meeting on resources that we were both attending. He was to speak at the meeting. Alone from Britain, I was there as an invited journalist. There was excitement in the air, a feeling that, surely, everything would soon change for the better because the great 'problematique' of mankind was now clearly visible. The date is important for, hopefully, ideas can grow faster than populations.

Those were the early, heady days, before the United Nations Stockholm Conference on the Human Environment, before *Small is Beautiful* reached publication, somewhere in that misty optimistic period when new concepts for alternative societies were 'in the air' and the world was beginning to react to the early computer studies on the limits to growth. The characteristics of exponential curves were becoming understood and everywhere the parable of the lily, a mere dot on the pond but doubling its area every day, became suddenly important. There were complex debates about feed-back loops and the validity assumptions: in high places the problem of population growth was minimised by plugging in convenient but entirely notional future rates of demographic transition, while the problems of world food supply were erased by pointing to the enormous slack being created by growth of technological possibility.

This fragmentary manipulation, remedial tinkering designed to obscure important central concepts about the 'oneness' of the earth's complex fabric and the increasing evidence of its violation, distressed Fritz: "It seems almost beyond belief that, in a world dominated by economists, we still pursue policies which squander or destroy the capital that we know to be essential for our survival", he said. This turned out to be the theme of his paper at the conference. It carried the day. The tragedy was that those who should have understood it most clearly chose to ignore it.

There were about four billion people on the planet at that time. In 1986, seemingly unnoticed, world population rose above the five billion mark without significant reduction in the overall exponential growth rate. The parable of the lily has become an awful reality. Yet it is local agricultural surpluses, not the evidence of soil erosion, or global starvation, or the destruction of world forests, or the rising levels of contamination, or the increasing damage through resource conversion, which remains the major—even the only—perceived trigger for political action. While the crises of resources, of human purpose and of non-sustainability, point to the all-pervasive unity of the problem, the great nations ignore reality and indulge, instead, in the schizophrenic and escapist fantasy of Star Wars.

Institutional inflexibility of Government and such fierce monsters as the 'military-industrial-political complex'—against which Eisenhower warned the world all those years ago—are still driving us blindly and at increasing speed over natural thresholds. Ordinary people, for the most part, yearn for stability, sustainability and the peace within which to express the deeper aspects of the human spirit. Yet they are enmeshed in the overriding context of 'hard' technology, of massive developments which not only dwarf natural systems and dehumanise humanity, but engender and express gross insensitivity toward human dignity and the fate of all living systems.

Evidence of damage is now worldwide. Slowly, the philosophy of development based on 'appropriate technology' is beginning to find a major niche. But the tide has not yet turned toward resource sustainability nor is there wide evidence of a shift toward a world in which the values of integrity, service, fulfilment, happiness and other non-material concepts are given high priority within this sustainable context. Yet there are signs of change. Everywhere people sense that our present way of doing things is not only wrong but leading toward disaster on a planetary scale. An understanding that natural and sympathetic approaches are right and that manipulation is wrong, is spreading.

This book, by explaining in a direct and powerful way why things are wrong and what could be done to transform society and its goals, will accelerate the process and may be crucially important to the future of our civilisation. It will certainly help to generate such pressure at the grass roots that the statesmen of the world will have to listen. I hope so. Mankind is at the point of destroying his own essential and natural basis for survival. There is a race between new ideas and old. If men do not change their ways then disaster will certainly do it for them. This book embodies a prescription for change that is based, not on disaster, but on sensitivity and clear perception. These are rare virtues.

Anthony Tucker
Science Correspondent
The Guardian

London
February 1987

Introduction

We were having a vegetarian Indian lunch in London with Satish Kumar. It was a lively meal. Satish was eloquent with new-age enthusiasm, and we were at our most sceptical. He was arguing that the topics that fill the pages of the magazine *Resurgence,* which he edits, all form part of a single movement. We disagreed; these topics range far too widely. They include 'small-is-beautiful' economics, human-scale education, organic farming, whole food, deep ecology, complementary medicine, Eastern and Western mysticism and much besides.

We said there was no such movement; it was all bits and pieces and people picked up whatever they fancied. We argued that a woman who bakes her own bread with organic flour may also deal in the stockmarket, smother her windows in frilly lace curtains and be a fully paid-up member of the consumer society. A man whose doctor fails to cure his backache may try acupuncture and work in a bank and run two cars. A mother looking for a smaller school for her child may have no wish to change the curriculum.

This book is our repentance. In the argument with Satish, both sides were right. This movement of ideas does not yet form a coherent ideology like Marxism, Conservatism, or Buddhism. You cannot call yourself a 'new age' thinker and expect people to understand what you mean. Yet there is a new world view which is breaking through the rigid structures of worn out thinking, like grass coming up between the cracks of paving-stones. People are beginning to accept parts of it, yet even when they wish to go further and adopt a less consumerist, more ecological lifestyle, they can't do so all at once; the paving-stones of official society form a solid and secure pavement. But Satish insists, and we now agree, that these ideas do form a movement and, within the movement, they relate with each other as parts of a whole.

That word 'whole' sums up the movement. What these ideas have in common is that they are holistic—a word which is more usefully spelled wholistic, because it means whole rather than holy. In this book, from now on, we shall spell it our way, even though as we shall argue later, something holy is implied in the word as well.

Wholistic thinking attempts to understand, as parts of a whole, subjects which in our society are usually kept separate. This separation is where our civilisation has gone wrong; everything has been compartmentalised. We have tried to do our religion on Sunday, our economics on Monday, and so on. Our economists have assumed that consumers and producers are different entities from people; our doctors have tried to cure backache without reference to heartache.

How can we understand the whole? Is it not impossibly hard to grasp, too vague to define, let alone talk to other people about? Surely we are dealing with an abstract philosophy or religion? No, the whole is not a high-falutin' concept. It is what we feel and think, the myriad of sensations, intuitions and rational thoughts which make up everyday consciousness. We need to rethink our education, economics and agriculture as though the 'whole of us' is concerned in each activity - not just the part of us which goes to school, buys, sells, eats or grows food. That is why people in this movement of ideas are looking for schools that are not separated from the people who live in the neighbourhood; for a kind of working and trading that involves more than money; a kind of farming that involves more than providing crops.

If you are a scientist, you are also a father or mother, husband or wife; perhaps a gardener, a traveller, a consumer, a music-lover, a Jew. That is your whole person. If there is a difficult abstraction here, it is the so-called reality which scientists have been taught to dissect and make theories about. As long as they remember that their theories are abstractions, representing only a fraction of human consciousness, there is no problem. Trouble arises when society begins to assume that scientific theories are reality. In our actual experience, reality is infinitely richer, infinitely complex.

Science cannot explain those aspects of reality which, when we speak of them, we call love, beauty, purpose, meaning. These are not words often heard in public, because that is not how society is organised. We have neither been taught nor encouraged to express feelings. Our civilisation has put everything which concerns reason and science on one shelf—the top shelf reserved for objective matters properly discussed in public; and intuition, feeling, love, beauty, sense of purpose and faith, on another, lower down—the shelf kept for subjective emotions which are private and therefore less important.

This separation of rational thought from feeling allows our officials to argue that we need nuclear power in spite of the risk of another Chernobyl catastrophe; to speak of defence in terms of nuclear weapons; and to confuse economic wellbeing with economic growth. If they could 'only connect', as E.M.Forster once pleaded. This failure to connect is the deepest reason why we are heading for trouble, whether it be nuclear war, famine or environmental disaster.

We agree with Satish that people are not just sitting back and waiting for the bang. There is after all, a movement—a movement of ideas increasingly expressed in action. What shall we call it? People involved often speak of new age thinking; they also talk of a new paradigm or mind-set. We shall use these terms sparingly, for they have been overdone. It is easy to pick out people who agree with us, and to say 'the world view has changed'. In the past, paradigm changes have not been reliably apparent until long after they have happened.

Shall we call our movement alternative?. That would be to confuse it with the hippies and flower people of the sixties. Their romantic enthusiasm has vanished. The movement of the eighties is not for dropouts; it wants to be considered part of the mainstream. It is significant that what used to be alternative medicine has come in from the cold and is now complementary medicine. Doctors with medical degrees have formed the British Holistic Medical Association. Whole food, a sophisticated fad in the sixties, has become one of today's few growth industries. In the sixties, the hippies were not concerned with famine in the third world; today many schoolchildren care and many try to help. Children also worry about the nuclear arms race and the implications of Chernobyl. On television, they can watch the destruction of tribal peoples, wildlife, plant species, forests and lakes. The world feels smaller and more dangerous. Our urgent need of remedies brings many sixties' rebels into today's movement—twenty years older and wiser.

So what shall we call our movement? Human-scale thinking is promising, but that might seem to narrow the question down to one of size, which is only a part of what we are trying to say. Wholistic thinking encompasses the widest range of meaning. That was not a phrase Fritz Schumacher used, but it is the key to his thinking—and his ideas now form a pivotal centre for the movement. Schumacher's protest against the 'bigger-is-better' mentality, which some of his followers call 'growthmanship', had behind it a long tradition of human-centred revolt against the industrial ethos. In *Small is Beautiful* and his other books, Schumacher was aiming, above all, to restore the lost links between economic man and a human being. His ideas have been developed by others as they relate to economics, technology, education, health, third world development and many other subjects.

These advocates of wholism do not operate in a vacuum. Their ideas are relevant because public confidence in the official view of the world is crumbling. When the horrors of the Vietnam War were shown on American television, the war could not be carried on because in part, of public revulsion. Now the horrors of our civilisation are on television too—old people freezing to death in rich societies, food mountains growing while people starve. In a rich country like Britain, economic life has come to assume the logic of *Alice in Wonderland;* millions of unemployed people moulder in costly idleness while houses need to be built, schools and hospitals want staff, sewers and railway stations fall into disrepair. One third of Britain's population lack what the other two-thirds consider essentials of living, while manipulators of money producing nothing, are enriched faster and more easily than ever before.

Socialists blame this scabrous situation on the capitalist system. Yet in many democratic countries in Europe as well as in the United States, people have voted the Right into power. Many of us distrust the Left because it offers no escape from the assumptions and rules of established society. Meanwhile, more and more people feel that they have become prisoners of an industrial, materialist world that respects no ideology and has swept away their ability to subsist on their own, to help themselves and even to think for themselves. We live in a rational, scientific age, yet the world no longer makes sense. Change has become imperative.

What that change implies, in theory and practice, will be the subject of this book. Does it mean going back to a simpler lifestyle? To some extent, yes; the world's goodies are not inexhaustible. But a simpler life can be a richer one. We shall need to rediscover human values, dignity and autonomy that have been lost in the onward rush for economic growth. We shall need to regain control—of ourselves first, our health, our education and our immediate communities, all of which have been colonised by the mass societies in which we live. Only then can we think of breaking through to another society—and that will be triumphantly new.

We have written this book together. It is the most wholistic thing we have ever done. We don't travel by bicycle like Jonathon Porritt; we don't live on a smallholding like Satish Kumar and June Mitchell. We live in the country, unlike Jonathon, bake our own bread and try to grow our own vegetables. But Walter works in London—though not in a bank. One of our five children is a firm vegetarian at the age of 17, another is proud of wire-cutting at missile bases; the most we can claim for them is that they are aware of values other than those that are dominant in consumer society. In writing the book together, we hoped at least to save it from macho thinking, which is at the opposite pole from wholistic and is, as we shall argue later, one of our culture's most basic errors. None of the chapters were written exclusively by either of us. A wholistic book should really have no chapters; we put them in as a concession to our education and yours. But you may start at the end or the middle and go backwards or forwards.

We wrote this book for people like ourselves, who hope to live into the twenty-first century but whose active working lives will have been spent in the nerve-wracking twentieth, and for our children's generation, growing up in this century but who will have their active working lives in the next one. Will they be able to develop those elements in our legacy which favour life, or must they rush on to more destruction?

We believe the wholistic approach to society, which is gradually breaking through, presents the best hope of surviving our global predicament. If like one of our sons, the threat of nuclear war preoccupies you, we hope to show how wholistic thinking if widely and wisely adopted, would eliminate that threat. We believe the wholistic approach is the right solution for the two other major problems - famine and environmental damage. That is a grand claim. We believe it can be substantiated.

CHAPTER ONE

A World View

Wenlock Edge, Shropshire from near Hatley Village, Denis Thorpe, The Guardian

A World View

SOME of the assumptions on which our civilisation is based are dead, others are sick and will not long survive. Yet much of our official and public life continues as though they were still valid. Inevitably this creates tension. Here are a few of these assumptions:

• That large organisations (firms, government departments, power stations, schools etc.) are more effective than small ones.
• That an essential purpose of an economic system is to provide at least one full-time paid job for every household.
• That an economy, however large, can only prosper if it continues to grow.
• That industrial societies provide the most promising model for the rest of the world and that economic aid enables the third world to develop.
• That the principal purpose of education is to open the way to a full-time paid job for life.
• That the best way to a healthier society is to provide more hospitals, more doctors and more medical machines.
• That the earth is an unlimited source of raw materials and an infinite receptacle for waste.

• That one country's economy and ecology can be kept separate from another's.
• That God is male.
• That knowledge is only valid if it is scientifically proven and that emotion is a less valid criterion for action than reason.

A few people speak out against these propositions; some of their counter-propositions are set out at the beginning of the next chapter. Many more people have doubts on at least some of the official propositions, but lack confidence or knowledge to express them. The result is the doubts are repressed and that leads to gloom, pessimism and neurosis. A strong current of nihilism has indeed been observed in many industrial countries, especially Britain. The British theologian, Lesslie Newbigin, observed when he came back after a long stay in the third world:

> Even in the worst slums in Madras, there always seemed to be the idea that there is something better ahead. Whereas, coming back to this country, I felt that middle-aged people were just hoping to keep reasonably comfortable until they had to go to the crematorium, and many young people had no expectation of anything beyond the nuclear holocaust. (1)

Depression, even among the affluent, fills doctors' surgeries and hospital wards. General practitioners and hospital doctors alike confirm that a high proportion of 'patients' are lonely, alienated, or without purpose. They have lost control of their lives. Dorothy Rowe, a clinical psychologist, suggests that the fear of nuclear war was only part of the anguish; the general background of depression is so pervasive that fear of war can serve as an emotional excuse.

> So many young people, I find, construe their future in 'as if' terms. 'If I am still alive next year or the year after, then I

might be finishing college.' Their future has a conditional, unreal quality which my future never had. I thought this was very sad—until I realised that such a way of thinking about the future was a defence against depression. If the future is not real then you won't feel resentful about being robbed of it. (2)

Many people appear happy enough on the surface but admit, often unexpectedly, that deep down they see society as a sham. They rarely refer directly to nuclear war, but often hint that at the back of their minds they see this as a logical nemesis of the way society is organised. We were having a cup of tea with Nick Sparks, the engineer who had come to install a telephone, when we began talking about this book. He said, "the problem is money. Money has lost its original meaning. Our managers are all accountants. They worry only about money and know nothing about the real business. I can't see any way of drastic change unless there was a global disaster." Nick Sparks felt he could not change anything. Perhaps people have always felt that, but it is ironical that the feeling should be prevalent in a a highly developed country which is also a democracy. Finance, big business and technology appear quite beyond our grasp. The officials associated with defence, health, etc. seem as remote, incomprehensible and all-powerful as the gods in the ancient world. The wishes of the gods were interpreted by the high priests, whilst the people remain ignorant.

It cannot be unconnected to this perplexity that, on both sides of the Atlantic, drug addiction should have approached epidemic proportions and alchoholism is rampant even among the young. The United States has between eleven and twenty million full-time alchoholics and an average of seventy people a day commit suicide, while another one thousand people try to do so.

Opinion polls show increasingly widespread disengage-ment by young people from politics, yet there is growing concern among all age groups over the general direction of society. Fifty-three per cent of Americans agreed in one poll that there was 'something deeply wrong with America' while forty-five per cent declared that 'the quality of life has deteriorated in the last 10 years'. Another poll found that seventy-two per cent believed government was run 'on behalf of a few special interests'. (3)

Fortunately not everyone is in despair. Millions of people in the third world and industrial societies have adopted small-scale initiatives which are inspired by the world view that will be outlined in this book. One survey found that more than a third of people in many developed countries reject the established aspirations of the industrial era in favour of post-industrial 'inner-directed values'. This, perhaps optimistic, report found these 'new people' added up to thirty-six per cent of Britons and Danes, as many as forty-seven per cent of the Dutch, twenty-six per cent of West Germans but only nineteen per cent of Americans and ten per cent of Japanese. (4)

In the United States the Stanford Institute has also studied 'inner-directed' Americans. The American writer, Duane Elgin, has praised the philosophy of such people, whom he estimates as ten million and who have opted for what he calls 'voluntary simplicity'. (5)

In every age the dominant world view has been challenged, but today's revulsion from official values has unprecedented urgency. Our ability to exterminate our species and most others by nuclear war and the wholesale destruction of the natural world that has already begun, is unique in world history. Also unique for our species is our enormous increase in numbers and the effect on the food supply. These threats are beginning to drive home to people, not just specialists, the knowledge that humanity can no longer afford to live by carelessly rushing onwards, crying 'more and more' and 'bigger and bigger'.

Much of the drama is revealed in a new global

consciousness which enables us, as no previous generation, to see the wholeness of our world's predicament. We are the first generation to have journeyed away from the earth and to have observed and photographed it as a unit.

We are the first generation to have consciously experienced a world energy crisis and a global pollution problem. We have lived through Chernobyl. The accident at the nuclear reactor in the Ukraine was caused by human error and can therefore happen again. On that occasion scores of people were killed, hundreds, perhaps thousands more are expected to die later and millions of hectares of agricultural land all over Europe were contaminated with radioactivity. The next accident could be much worse. Chernobyl produced a powerful wave of doubt about the value of nuclear energy throughout the developed world. Behind the doubts lay an unspoken question: if our way of life needs so much energy that nuclear power is essential in spite of its horrific risks, what is wrong with our way of life? The Chernobyl accident was followed by official evasions, bland reassurance that 'it could not happen here'—thereby providing fresh insight into the secretive and irresponsible way authority can be exercised in our societies.

This is also the first time that a large segment of the population has been made to feel permanently irrelevant through unemployment. The depression of the 1930's had none of this permanency. The claim by political parties that they can bring the jobs back by their various recipes sounds hollow and only adds to the general sense of unreality and alienation. A profound misuse of ability is apparent; a redundant population is idly incarcerated in cities, while a nation's social services and infrastructure are in desperate need of manning and repair and the countryside remains unpeopled. The modern predicament was expressed in fantasy in Robert van de Weyer's book, *Wickwyn - a Vision of the Future*, the story of the English village from the Middle Ages to the 21st century:

All alike found themselves in the same dilemma: on the one hand the new technology offered the prospect of high living standards for all humanity; on the other hand a growing proportion of humankind found itself useless and redundant, unable to share in the production or the enjoyment of this prosperity. The physical and social structure in which people lived incarcerated them...At the material level...people were unable to organise themselves to use this technology to their mutual benefit...At the spiritual level,...they were unable within the context of the old industrial cities to create a more shared, personal way of life in co-operation with others. (6)

In Van de Weyer's story, the tide turns just about now, after centuries of rural decay. The new ideology which emerges leads towards a rejuvenated, repopulated village with small local industries, windmills for extra power, locally run schools and hospitals, parish-scale local government and self-reliance. People who were unemployed could grow food and start a small business: those in jobs "sought to reduce their working hours to follow a similar course, combining part-time employment with a greater amount of time working at home".

One reason for disenchantment with the official world view is that something has gone wrong with economic development. After four decades of this process, eight hundred million people—a sixth of the world—today eat fewer than the calories deemed essential for an 'active working life', according to official international reports. Half of these eat at a level insufficient to prevent 'stunted growth and serious health risks'. (7) Even by the official yardsticks of development many countries in Africa are going backwards— and suffering famines which can often be directly linked to the destruction of grazing lands in the name of development. Comforting global figures show that world food production increased at an annual rate of 2.2 per cent during the decade after 1973—almost 0.5 per cent faster than population growth. But in the least developed thirty-six countries, the rate of food production increase at 2.1 per cent was fully half a percentage point below their population growth. Despite increasing world production, over a billion people are excluded by poverty from the food market. (8)

The classic success story has hitherto been the fall in infant mortality. Now even this has been reversed in a score of food deficit countries, especially in Africa, where aid officials and experts can be heard talking of regions 'going back to the bush' or 'becoming a desert'.

Officials place the main blame for continuing poverty and hunger on population growth; yet it is increasingly obvious that population cannot be effectively checked until people are involved in their own development. Until poor people have the security of a viable economic life, children are their chief source of security. Who else can provide for them in their old age ?

The correct conclusion to draw from this situation is that the third world and the rich world have the same need: restoring people's involvement. Meanwhile misguided government policies, ill-conceived 'aid' and disappointments with the results of 'scientific' methods of agriculture, are as much to blame as population growth. Even the famed 'green revolution' in agriculture has run into serious problems, including pest resistance, the need for more and more fertiliser, shortage of water for irrigation and the marginalization of peasant farmers.

Some aspects of 'development' now threaten the health of the whole world—especially the onslaught by speculators and profiteers on tropical forests. Between twenty-five and forty per cent of the original extent of the tropical forests had already been lost by 1980 and a current estimate is that about eighty thousand square kilometres—an area the size of Austria—is lost, that is, converted to non-forest uses each year. By the year 2000 at that rate, about twelve per cent of moist and ten per cent of dry tropical forests, remaining in 1980, will be gone. In addition to the immediate catastrophe for the people living in and around the forests, whose traditional subsistence economies are shattered, this has serious implications for the world's climate, because tropical forests help cool the earth. It is also a catastrophe for millions of species of plant life which are vital for plant breeding and medicine. At current rates of tropical forest loss, a million species—ten-twelve per cent of the earth's total—could become extinct by the year 2000. Most will disappear without ever having been discovered. Also, the very soil needed to grow food is disappearing under the strain of development. Desertification has damaged three billion hectares—almost one quarter of the earth's land surface.

With such results the very concept of development, which is supposed to be promoted by aid and trade, is now being challenged.In theory, developing countries must trade to pay for the essential inputs of development and to repay the debts incurred by aid; in practice, these countries are forced to grow export crops at the expense of the food production they need to feed their own people.The production of export crops is also at the expense of their natural environment. The situation is made worse by steadily falling prices of raw materials and rising prices for manufactures, giving the third world a worse bargain than ever. Why should peasants grow cotton, coffee and cocoa, which they cannot eat, to pay for luxuries for their governing classes and to finance investment in heavy industries producing goods the poor cannot buy? The main hope for a more equitable form of development lies in the revolt from conventional methods of aid. The need is for development 'from below', through intermediate technology and community-based projects. We need an end to projects like gigantic dams that displace local people, alter natural habitats, aid salination and spread water-borne diseases. The main benefit of such dams goes to the multinational companies that set up industries using cheap electricity and cheap labour, further destroying the environment and the local culture. (9)

In raising all these questions, we are involved in an exercise of locating what went wrong—not with capitalism or socialism but the basic dynamic of our civilisation and its threefold rush towards war, environmental destruction and mass starvation. Rudolf Bahro is a radical critic of capitalist economies. He is a former Marxist who became a Green. Bahro has called this basic dynamic 'exterminism', suggesting that this culture "which announced its birth in *The Iliad*, has been exterminist in its most inner dispositions, modelling itself on individual competition and the Olympian principle of 'more, higher, faster, better'." Bahro concludes that without a cultural revolution we have no chance against the arms race because our perspective is quite wrong. "The foundations deep in the European soil are warlike...people voted Kohl because they wanted to keep up their living standard. They were well aware that he would also bring in the missiles, but that was a third rate question for them..."(10)

Seen in relation to the timespan of human history, the scientific and materialist view of the world is of recent origin. It is barely four centuries old—and has only been dominant for a century or two. Scientific materialism grew out of a synthesis of the scientific revolution of the 17th century and the ideas of the Enlightenment. Descartes' philosophy taught us to separate our own inner perceptions from the supposedly objective external world. Newton's science sought to reduce nature to its supposed building blocks, which were thought originally to be atoms. Modern medicine took the same reductionist line, aiming to identify and treat diseases as though they had an existence separate from the patient as a whole. Economics and sociology followed a similar tradition, explaining the workings of society as one might explain a clockwork machine. This ordered, rational view of the world was revised but not superseded when Darwin explained evolution in terms of blind, competing forces. The Darwinian concept of the survival of the fittest coincided with the growth of industry—a biological idea tailor-made for industrial society.

The brave new world of science and industry indeed provided us—well, some of us—with undreamed of prosperity and personal freedom. But today the fruits of scientific materialism look less appetizing. Industrial society once promised us a job, but no longer honours the promise. Our food is poisoned, our rivers and lakes polluted. Acid rain kills our temperate forests, while our tropical forests are cut down at the rate of thousands of hectares daily. Welsh lambs are contaminated with Russian radioactivity. The superpowers threaten us with a nuclear holocaust, 'Star Wars' is the pinnacle of technology in the world's richest country and meanwhile, eight hundred million people—a sixth of the world—remain grievously underfed. In a world like that, one is naturally prone to be curious about what scientific rationalism leaves out.

And this is the moment in history when science itself appears to have reached the frontiers of materialism. Relativity and quantum physics suggest that matter is not solid after all; nor can we any longer be sure that it exists independently of our minds. Matter is interchangeable with energy. Laboratory experiments have demonstrated that the observer, merely by observing, can affect the behaviour of matter. Scientists have observed one subatomic particle interacting with another, with no scientifically known contact between them. The 'laws' of physics have been amended.

The new physics does not prove that scientific method has been misconceived; still less does it prove the existence of God. But an essential dialogue has been reopened between physics and metaphysics. The smug certainties implicit in Western dualism with its separation of mind and matter have been eroded. Reductionist experiments remain a valid method of study, but they are no longer adequate to explain the physical world. Eastern philosophies and folk wisdom, which Westerners have arrogantly dismissed as primitive or unscientific, begin to appeal even to scientists. The way forward seems to lie in a wholism which includes traditional wisdom.

Another fundamental flaw in our culture, as we shall see in chapter eleven, is that it is male-dominated—not only in the domination of women by men, but in the primacy of reason over feeling. We have equated reason with masculine qualities and feeling with feminine qualities. Men as well as women are now led to criticize this macho culture, realizing that both sexes are equal losers. These critics point out that women's theoretical status of equality continues to be ignored in the scramble for work, where they remain at the lowest end of the scale in temporary, low-paid jobs. In Britain the movement for the ordination of women, while directly affecting only a small minority, invokes a passionate response among men as well as women. If women are excluded from office by the Church, the highest moral institution, could they hope for better consideration elsewhere? Here again, a surface issue masks a deeper one: the macho culture that fails to respect women also fails to respect the earth. The same culture exploits the third world and conducts the nuclear arms race.

We are living in a patriarchal society, which typically respects man-made law, rational thought and sustained effort to control and change the natural world. Erich Fromm has pointed out that matriarchal society, in contrast, is character-ised by the importance of blood ties, close links with the land and acceptance of human dependence on nature. (11)

Our macho culture strikes James Robertson, a leading writer on post-industrial thinking, as unhealthy: "the masculine and feminine have split so far apart, and the masculine has come to dominate the feminine so much, that it is hardly too much to feel that we now live in a nightmare fantasy world. The nightmare is all too real: the outcome could be the nuclear holocaust." (12)

Will the world view change? The last major change—the discovery of Copernicus that the earth went round the sun and not the other way round—took one hundred and fifty years to become culturally absorbed. David Pepper, an historian of green thinking, explains why this took so long. The new ideas of the 17th century served:

> Not only as an intellectual challenge to the established science. They also ate away at the theology from which it stemmed—which in turn supported a particular social structure. And were it not for the social and economic challenges to that structure which, too, were being made, it is doubtful whether the intellectual ideas represented by the Newtonian paradigm would have triumphed in the 18th and 19th centuries as they did. (13)

By that criterion, all the elements are in place for change today: this time it will certainly not take one hundred and fifty years.

Notes:

(1) Lesslie Newbigin, *The Turn of The Tide.*

(2) Dorothy Rowe, interview with the authors, 1985. See also, *Living with the Bomb*, (RKP 1985).

(3) Kirkpatrick Sale, *Human Scale*, page 24-25.

(4) Taylor Nelson, *Monitor Study for the National Economic Development Office* 1986, Peter Large, *The Guardian* 7/2/86.

(5) Duane Elgin, *Voluntary Simplicity*, page 126-133.

(6) Robert Van de Weyer, *Wickwyn*, pages 17 & 23.

(7) *World Resources* 1986, page 1.

(8) FAO *State of Food & Agriculture*, 1984.

(9) Edward Goldsmith and Nicholas Hildyard, *The Social and Environmental Effects of Large Dams*, see also Janet Mohun and Omar Sattuar, *The Drowning of a Culture*, *New Scientist* 15/1/87, pages 37-42.

(10) Rudolf Bahro, *Building the Green Movement.*

(11) Erich Fromm, *The Sane Society*.

(12) James Robertson, *Future Work*.

(13) David Pepper, *The Roots of Modern Environmentalism.*

CHAPTER TWO

Breaking Through

Winter Wheat Emerging Through the Snow, © Rosemary and Penelope Ellis

Breaking Through

THOSE of us who wish to replace the materialist and consumerist values of our society with more wholistic values are not planning revolution, and most of us have no greenprint for political action. Our action is individual and local; we are reacting with small initiatives against the corrupt, aggressive and expansionist elements of our society. These initiatives can appear to be very different in their nature; at first sight there is not much in common between an inner city theatre project, a Devon goat farm or a save-the-dolphin campaign. However, we share some assumptions; here are just a few:

• That our first priority, in the industrial as well as the third world, is to regain control of our lives—our subsistence, our health, our work, our environment, the education of our children and our cultural life.
• That we must act locally to restore vitality to our extended families (including grandpa, grandma and lots of others) and our neighbourhoods; and think globally so that our consumption of food, energy and raw materials is in harmony with global resources and needs.
• That our work is primarily done for ourselves, our families

and neighbourhoods.
• That the playful and the festive must return to our lives, in rituals, carnivals and festivals.
• That the arts are the expression of our own creativity and we are more than the recipients of commercial entertainment.
• That men and women should practise real, not assumed, equality in private as well as public.
• That health is not the absence of disease, nor can it be bestowed by the state, by doctors or by hospitals. Our health is our right relationship with our bodies, families, communities and environment.
• That schools should be operated with the help of the local community.
• That our locality is part of a bio-region and we must learn to respect the ecology of both. Land is not only a source of food but is also for spiritual nourishment. Our city must be good to live in.
• That the sacred and the spiritual have a part in our lives.

But this is theory: the best way to join the new society is through action. Opportunities are increasing in spite of and because of the recession. When we're jobless, we can still work. We can join a co-operative, a community business or an enterprise workshop; these exist in every town. We can help improve, enliven or humanise our neighbourhood; exploit our hobbies and talents and bring them into the mainstream of our lives. We can try to raise money by applying for grants or loans for an approved local or national scheme: there is often money available if we know where to look. Once there's some cash, a business can start in partnership with one or two friends. Even people who have got a job can find some of these activities rewarding for part of the time. Whatever is going on in our neighbourhood can be linked up with what is happening elsewhere. This is called networking and this, too, is part of the new society.

Those of us with jobs, have other options for breaking through. When we grow exasperated with conformist consumer society, we join others who live better, growing some of our own food. If we don't have a garden, we can join an allotment; if there isn't one, we start one. When we can no longer bear the flabbiness of factory bread—we bake our own. When we're angry about our local school closing down, why don't we get together with neighbours and start a community school? It has been done. Neighbours will help buy it or build it. The children may well cook their own dinner, a useful skill to learn at school. Local people will be ready to give some lessons, on subjects they know more about than teachers. In such a school, unemployed people and pensioners find purpose and interest.

Action, not manifestos, is the starting point for green living: the grassroots economy exists, is expanding and, according to the new economists and philosophers, destined to become the norm.

When we feel our savings are paying for remote and pernicious activities like propping up apartheid, polluting rivers or sustaining the arms race, we can invest them locally to benefit our own community and employ our neighbours. Specialised investment companies exist that put our money in ecologically sound ventures; we shall describe them in the next chapter.

When large-scale farming disgusts us because it ruins the landscape, kills wildlife, pollutes water and produces tasteless food—we can buy organically grown food from our local health shop. There's one on nearly every High Street. If there isn't one, we can start one. Those of us living in a town and wanting to grow vegetables, can garden evenings and weekends on a city farm. There are city farms in many large towns, but if there isn't one, nothing stops us setting one up. A national organisation is there to help (see chapter four). Anyone can try permaculture on the balcony (a form of intensive gardening we describe in chapter nine).

This green way of doing has a negative starting point, based on a rejection of a discredited economic system. Rebels are voting with their feet. Some reject consumer society and live in rural communes or co-operatives. Others are driven to explore new lifestyles, or rediscover old ones.

These strategies are not rural dreams of return to Arcadia. They happen also in cities, where most people in the industrial world live. The essential idea is to act for ourselves, not waiting for 'them' to hand us jobs, services and amenities. In Britain these ideas may sometimes sound like the radical conservatism of the Thatcher government. The resemblance is deceptive and superficial; human-scale economics goes much further and deeper, and moves in a different direction from Thatcherism. Freedom is sought from the bureaucracy of the multinational as well as the state, from the tyranny of the Central Electricity Generating Board as well as the Area Health Service.

Our purpose is restoring to a community the human and natural resources it once had, which were lost in the homogenising effect of industrial society. We start by decolonising—first ourselves and then our community. A town or a village which depends on a single coal mine for its livelihood, is equally as colonized as a Ghanaian or Brazilian village producing nothing but cocoa or coffee for export. The villagers can't eat cocoa and coffee beans, any more than they can eat coal.

In Britain and Canada, this self-help message has been spread by Guy Dauncey, an itinerant 'barefoot' economist who specialises in inner-city revival. Dauncey has travelled from one decayed city to another, putting people in touch, networking and discussing the philosophical implications of a change to the human-scale. His battered address-book has long been the best sourcebook in Britain of new economics. Dauncey explained to a meeting of The Other Economic Sumnmit (TOES) in 1985 :

Unless a community contains a wide range of varied, locally owned and controlled business, it stands at the mercy of the international tradewinds, which can destroy a monocrop economy overnight, and the policy makers of Tokyo and New York, who can close down a local branch even without properly knowing where it is.... The alienation from our own local economies, which makes us feel that we cannot do anything about unemployment, also makes us feel unable to do anything about famines overseas and the gradual destruction of the earth's atmosphere.

Dauncey's themes modernise the ideas of Fritz Schumacher, who first formulated the current revolt against industrial economics—first on ecological grounds and later, as his thought developed, on human and spiritual grounds. Schumacher worked at the National Coal Board; *Small is Beautiful* was written before the first oil crisis, which Schumacher anticipated, taking the senseless depletion of fossil fuels as the starting point of his arguments:

The modern industrial system, with all its intellectual sophistication consumes the very basis on which it has been erected. To use the language of the economist it lives on irreplaceable capital which it cheerfully treats as income... I have taken fuel merely as an example to illustrate a very simple thesis: that economic growth, which viewed from the point of view of economics, physics, chemistry and technology, has no discernable limit, must necessarily run into decisive bottlenecks when viewed from the point of view of the environmental sciences...... An attitude to life which seeks fulfillment in the singleminded pursuit of wealth—in short, materialism—does not fit into this world, because it contains within itself no limiting principle, while the environment in which it is placed is strictly limited. Already the environment is trying to tell us that certain stresses are becoming excessive. As one problem is 'solved,' ten new problems arise as a result of the first 'solution'. (1)

Such views, expressed in the 1970s, were considered unorthodox and revolutionary. Now they are becoming platitudes. In the Worldwatch Institute's *State of the World* report for 1985, the directors, Lester R. Browne and Edward C. Wolfe, said the main need was:

> ...the realisation that our security and future wellbeing may be threatened less by the conflicts among nations than they are by the deteriorating relationship between ourselves, soon to be five billion, and the natural systems and resources that sustain us.

Such a re-orientation would have to include 'economic and population policies that respect the carrying capacity of local ecosystems, protect soils, and preserve biological diversity.' It would include planting trees, conserving soil and water, reducing CO_2 build-up, slowing population growth, increasing energy efficiency and recycling materials.

New economics began as a critique of large political and economic institutions by the Austrian economist and philosopher, Leopold Kohr:

> It is not poverty that is our problem, it is the vast spread of poverty. It is not unemployment but the dimension of modern unemployment which is a scandal: not hunger but the terrifying numbers affected by it: not depresssion but its world-encircling magnitude: not war but the atomic scale of war. (2)

Taking the example of the old city-state which one orator's voice could cover, Kohr moved on to advocate a "cantonised system of largely self-sufficient communities". Schumacher expanded that idea to include economic organisations and gave the movement a spiritual dimension by his excursion into 'Buddhist economics'. Translated into economic terms, the arguments against gigantism and macho-expansionist-exploitation of people and the natural environment were refined into a revolt against the notion of growth. At their annual meetings at the Alternative Economic Summit, TOES, where the new ideas are floated and discussed, wholistic economists began talking of growthmanship and growthmania.

Most new economists are ambivalent about growth; they tend to accept only 'good' growth. However, Herman Daly, professor of economics at Louisiana, gave TOES a sardonic and uncompromising 'steady state' lecture. The economy he advocates can "develop qualitatively but does not grow in quantitive style, just as the planet earth, of which human economy is a sub-system, develops without growing".

Neoclassical growth models notwithstanding, the surface of the earth does not grow at a rate equal to the rate of interest...When we add to the GNP the costs of defending ourselves against the unwanted consequences of growth, then we have hyper-growthmania. When we deplete the geological capital and ecological life-support systems and count that depletion as net current income, then we arrive at our present state of terminal hypergrowthmania.

The revolt against growth is at the heart of the conflict between what Erich Fromm has called the *having* and the *being* mode of existence. The first implies having more and more; the second means having what you need. Fromm sees the two concepts as the difference between "a society centred around persons and one centred around things".

New economics has taken from Marxism the restoration of the idea of needs and contributions—to each according to his need, from each acording his ability; from the Judaeo-Christian tradition comes the insistence on the moral responsibility of individuals. From this dual basis, new economists seek the appropriate attitude to needs and to wealth. Jonathon Porritt, Director of Friends of the Earth and an influential figure in the green movement, defines the problem:

> At the individual level today, wealth means the visible symbols of affluence. It means consumer durables and credit cards and being rich enough to have a huge overdraft. How, oh how, is this going to change in the new order? In a sustainable, ecological future, the wealthy will be those who have the independence and the education to enhance the real quality of their lives. The poor will be those who look back to an age where money might—but never quite did—buy happiness. The wealthy will be those who live and work in friendly, mutually supportive communities. The poor will be those still trucking off to cities. [3]

In this new economics, work becomes *ownwork*—a word coined by James Robertson. It is argued that the society which assesses a man's worth and status on the paid work he does is only as old as the industrial revolution. In a post-industrial age, this assessment is no longer justified. The jobs will never come back and anyway, we can find better things to do than work 40 hours a week for 40 weeks a year for 40 years in a lifetime. Ownwork is what we do that matters to us, whether it is remunerated or not. The range goes from housework to adult education, from practising the flute to helping out at a local enterprise agency. Ownwork includes all meaningful acitivity and that includes housework. Ownwork should be taken a-la-carte, with freedom to work part-time, to work in a paid job or at home, then perhaps a spell at university and a few years in a voluntary job.

Who pays for ownwork, and if we all do it, who is left to pay taxes? The answer of new economics is that the present expensive and stifling paraphernalia of dole and social security payments—which force people to be idle to qualify for their money—should be consolidated into a national basic wage. This guaranteed minimum income or social wage would be paid, as of right, with no questions asked to every man, woman and child, working or not as they please. This would liberate people to do the work they really want and the assumption is they would work much better than they do now.

Another part of new economics is what Schumacher called 'appropriate technology'. With his friend George McRobie, he founded the Intermediate Technology Group which still functions, advising both the industrial and the third world on how to avoid the sin of gigantism, to which governments of both the left and the right fall prey. He argued that the so-called economies of scale tend to disappear when measured against social costs. A small brickworks and a small power station—each exactly suited to its local raw materials and outlets, is better for society than its gigantic counterpart.

All these ideas should to be taught in human-scale schools. Here is another revolt against gigantism. It is a revolt also against a job-orientated, exam-structured system of education which is creating a generation of failures. The system is geared to universities, where less than one in ten of pupils go, and to jobs, which are no longer widely available. Schools are tending to concentrate on training rather than education. We are encouraged "to have knowledge as a possession, by and large commensurate with the amount of property or social prestige they are likely to have in later life". (4)

There can be no wholistic living without a return to human scale agriculture. There is a widespread and a growing dislike for large-scale and factory farming which leads to the environmental degradation of the countryside and its virtual depopulation. Human-scale farming must be organic farming, of which the products are already in rapidly growing demand. The current move away from the EEC's costly food mountains is fortunately opening the way for more diversified farming. It is more than a practical need: a society in tune with nature must restore to farming its spiritual element. It must sympathise with Thoreau's distate for the typical farmer he saw in New England in the last century:

> I respect not his labours, his farm where everything has its price, who would carry the landscape, who would carry his God to market, if he could get anything for him.... on whose farm nothing grows free.... whose fruits are not ripe for him till they are turned to dollars. Give me poverty that enjoys true wealth.

Healthy self-reliance as opposed to a sick dependency is the essential green-thinking objective and this applies to health itself. The new economists complain that society today counts health as a cost against economic progress, not an intrinsic economic aim. They complain that our so-called health service is really a sickness service; it mainly treats the symptoms of the sicknesses associated with industrial society. And it does this with the reductionist, mechanistic approach that has characterised human endeavour since the Enlightenment. In any case, economic dependency is not compatible with true health, as James Robertson argued at the 1985 TOES meeting:

> The conventional path of development creates dependency. Historically, it starts by excluding people from access to land, and therefore from a subsistence way of life. It thus makes people dependent on paid labour or cash handouts for the money to meet needs formerly met by ownwork. It goes on to make people dependant on organisations and professions to provide for all needs, including health needs.... This is an instance of the metaphysical assumption, derived originally from the philosophy of Descartes, and now underlying conventional science, that only the material, tangible, measurable side of the material/non-material duality can be scientifically understood. In the sphere of health this finds

expression in the idea that the human body is best understood as a machine...that health consists of the proper functioning of this machine, and that the way to improve its functioning is by intervention—e.g. by drugs, surgery, transplants—from outside. (4)

In the last resort the movement to a human-centred world must be understood as a spiritual movement, a modern synthesis between the spiritual and the material, which Erich Fromm outlines at the conclusion of *To Have or To Be?*.

Later medieval culture flourished because people followed the vision of the *City of God*. Modern society flourished, because people were energised by the vision of the growth of the *Earthly City of Progress*. In our century, however, this vision deteriorated to that of the *Tower of Babel*, which is now beginning to collapse and will, ultimately bury everybody in its ruins. If the City of God and the Earthly City were *thesis* and *antithesis,* a new *synthesis* is the only alternative to chaos: the synthesis between the spiritual core of the late medieval world and the development of rational thought and science since the Renaissance. This synthesis is *The City of Being.* (5)

Notes:

(1) E.F.Schumacher, *Small is Beautiful*, page 16.

(2) Leopold Kohr, *The Breakdown of Nations,* (Dutton 1978).

(3) Jonathon Porritt, *Green Politics*, quoted in Inglis, pages 26-27.

(4) James Robertson, TOES meeting, 1985.

(5) Erich Fromm, *To Have or To Be.*

CHAPTER THREE

New Economics

A Wholefood Shop, Denis Thorpe, The Guardian

New
Economics

NEW ECONOMICS is a radical revolt from the old, in
favour of what Schumacher called—in the subtitle of
Small is Beautiful—'a study of economics as if people
mattered'. It is human-centred and human-scaled—that is, it
offers a new perspective. In the foreground are people, not
consumers or producers; in the background is an ecologically
sound environment. Work is seen as human activity, not as a
commodity called labour.

The first premise is that industrial society, which
developed at the same time as modern economics, is now
itself regulated in large measure according to the precepts of
that science. Economic 'laws' have become as important as
laws enacted in our parliaments; growth, development,
monetarism and other notions have an assumed status as
high as moral precepts. Industrial society as we know it has
begun to falter—at least in part—because economic ideas
were flawed from the outset.

Economics counts money-measurable benefits and
costs, ignoring the human reality behind them. This accords
with the tenets of our industrial society, which has made a
marketable commodity not only of work, but of health, home,
food, education, leisure and even art. So the revolt against

economics is really a revolt against industrial society.

Instead of satisfying human needs, industrial society creates artificial desires. Since there must be growth, we have to buy more. Surrounded with purchased goods, we become dependent on them; we need to buy still more—and then we need to buy remedies against their ill effects. These effects include urban stress, exhaustion, depression and illness caused by pollution; and these maladies in turn compel us to become consumers of health services and holidays, thereby doing our duty by adding further to the gross national product.

From this starting point, the critique delves deeper, peeling off artificial layers of economic man's motivation in an attempt to rediscover what people really need. Erich Fromm, a major prophet of human-centred economic thinking, makes this point by asking the question *To Have or To Be?:* In industrial society we do not work, we 'have' a job; we are not healthy, we 'have' good health, and so on. As a result, "we are a society of notoriously unhappy people: lonely, anxious, depressed, destructive, dependent—people who are glad when we have killed the time we are trying so hard to save". (1)

Fromm rejects the principle, tacitly accepted by conventional economists, that the pursuit of individual economic interests adds up to welfare for the whole. Economists call this benign, mystic concept the 'hidden hand'. Fromm translates the principle into a psychological analysis of materialism and finds:

> . . . that I want everything for myself; that possessing, not
> sharing, gives me pleasure; that I must become greedy
> because if my aim is having, I *am* more the more I *have;* I
> must feel antagonistic towards all others: my customers
> whom I want to deceive, my competitors whom I want to
> destroy, my workers whom I want to exploit. I can never be
> satisfied, because there is no end to my wishes; I must be

envious of those who have more and afraid of those who have less. (2)

The new economics is radical, not in the left-wing sense but literally, in seeking to pull the old economics up by its roots. These roots have such names as gross national product, growth, economic development, economies of scale and division of labour. It also redefines demand, supply, production and consumption. Demand is defined as what people need and want as opposed to what they may be induced to buy. Production and supply are defined as the provision of goods and services which people need and want, which make long-term sense for the community, the bio-region and the world. The gross national product, an unreal measurement whose artificiality is regarded as highly pernicious, is replaced by a more meaningful measurement. The GNP calculation counts pollution and resource-depleting activities as part of 'growth,' while ignoring the activities, like child-rearing, gardening, house-improvement and voluntary work, that matter most in many peoples' lives. Mere growth for its own sake is replaced in the new economics by sustainable growth in the quality rather than the quantity of goods and services. Human and social development takes the place of economic development and appropriately-sized units of production replace gigantic corporations, factories, farms and power stations.

Conventional economists reply that they are criticised outside their competence; they profess only to deal in quantifiable wants and commodities, not spiritual matters like the quality of the environment, which they place under the heading of externalities. They claim that the laws of supply and demand are adequate to express and regulate economic activity; thus, if there is pollution, there will be demand for its eradication; if oil becomes too costly, demand will fall off, alternative energy sources will become economic and the problem will be solved.

New economists reply in their turn that this reasoning may have been alright for Adam Smith and Ricardo in the 18th century, but is no longer acceptable in a world shrunk by technology, a global village, whose boundaries are known and where there are no further frontiers.

In conventional views on capitalism, competition is supposed to ensure the smooth and fair working of the economy, but the inordinate growth of state power, itself overtaken by the power of multinational companies, has made a mockery of competition. When government can no longer take rational economic decisions, what chance is there for people?

Critics of the new economics say they detect authoritarian undertones, since someone has to determine what is ecologicaly sound—and enforce the ecological order on everybody. New economists reply that there is nothing more authoritarian than the remote corporations we have today, which open and close their factories without reference to national or local needs. In contrast, the new economics is designed to work for people who have regained their basic autonomy.

In America, a flourishing school of futurologists exists. One of its most distinguished members, Hazel Henderson, wrote: "It is no longer a matter of *who owns* the means of production, but the need to address the ecological, social and spiritual dilemmas posed by the means of production themselves." (3)

For a time and to an extent, economics worked as a way of interpreting and regulating the ceaseless and apparently limitless expansion of capitalist countries. But in today's finite and shrinking world, the science has become absurdly dated.

Economic beliefs originated in the new world of commerce which emerged from a society dominated by priests and aristocrats. The supremacy of the commercial classes over the old order, ensured that the new science was never morally neutral. Economics was, indeed, "biassed from the very start", as John Galtung argued at The Other Economic Summit of 1985:

> It liberates human beings from fear of punishment. As long as you play the game, you can enter the market; abide by the rules and you have a wide range of behaviour at your disposal, whether you are a willing buyer or a willing seller or both. (4)

THE ECONOMIES OF THE SMALL-SCALE

Today the new economics stands for the restoration of lost values, but not for ignoring technology. Nor is smallness valued in the abstract. The lost value sought is the acknowledgement of the appropriate: the factory that supplies regional needs and employs local people; the farmer who protects the environment, while providing good food and livelihood. Appropriate technology is no less modern or sophisticated than monster factories. What better tool than the micro-computer as a means of domestic and professional self-reliance? Victor Papenek in his brilliant book *Design for the Real World* which first appeared in 1971, gave numerous examples of appropriately designed technology; radios for the third world that cost a few cents, tools for disabled workers. Schumacher was very precise about the beauty of smallness:

> Experience shows that whenever you can achieve smallness, simplicity, capital cheapness and non-violence, or indeed any one of these objectives, new possibilities are created for people, singly or collectively, to help themselves, and that the patterns that result from such technologies are more humane, more ecological, less dependent on fossil fuels and closer to real human needs than the patterns created by technologies

that go for giantism, complexity, capital intensity, and violence. (5)

Schumacher conceded that the economies of scale had relevant application in the 19th century; but monster organisations became counter-productive through their very size, and today, our technology can make things small again. We have a long way to go.

> When you travel up the big motor road from London you find yourself surrounded by a huge fleet of lorries carrying biscuits from London to Glasgow. And when you look across to the other motorway, you find an equally huge fleet of lorries carrying biscuits from Glasgow to London. Any impartial observer from another planet would come to the inescapable conclusion that biscuits have to be transported at least six hundred miles before they reach their proper quality.(6)

Schumacher concedes that it is perfectly logical for the London manufacturer to send his surplus to Glasgow, since the cost of transport is only a fraction of the whole. Unfortunately, the Glasgow biscuiteer thinks the same and invades the London market. This makes economics so fascinating: what makes good business sense can in terms of the total sum become ridiculous. What makes the situation absurd in Schumacher's eyes is the large scale production of these biscuits, which in turn is a result of large accumulations of capital and cheap oil. He advocates small units, using a simplified technology. Similarly, he argues that what is needed, in poor countries even more than rich ones, is not one cement factory producing half a million tons of cement a year but a hundred plants scattered about where the resources are and where the demand is, to make a few thousand tons a year each.

AN END TO GROWTH AND A NEW GNP

The coming of age of the new economics in Britain was marked in 1986 by the publication of *The Living Economy*—an edited compilation of papers delivered at the first two annual sessions of The Other Economic Summit (TOES). These meetings are timed each year to coincide with the official world economic summit and TOES never forgets to deliver to the official meeting a resounding memorandum on human realities which economics ministers ignore.

The first line of attack is directed against the official assumption that the growth of the gross national product (GNP) measures a nation's economic wellbeing. This 'absurd arithmetic' applies all over the world, as Manfred Maxneef, the Chilian economist and witty critic of pseudo-development, told a new economics meeting:

The only sign that exists is plus; you can only add, never subtract. So any process that generates a monetary flux is acceptable. It is totally irrelevant whether it is productive, unproductive or destructive—it all adds to the GNP...If I want my GNP to grow in order to impress the IMF. If I am lucky enough to have a tremendous epidemic in my country, with my whole population getting sick and consuming a large amount of drugs, my GNP will also grow.

Maxneef drives home the illogicality of the GNP in his story of two women neighbours who are both tired of seeing the hard work they do in their houses unacknowledged in the national statistics. So they agree to clean each other's house and pay one another £500 a year, thus ensuring their work is counted in the GNP.

Hazel Henderson argues that a realistic GNP should reflect the social costs of economic activity, "i.e. publicly borne costs of the tobacco and alchohol industries, rising drug abuse costs attributable to drug companies and their advertising, health costs of tooth decay and poor nutrition due to promotion of oversweetened cereals and snacks, clean-up costs of polluted waters, costs of cancer related to environmental carcinogens, etc." (7) In the same spirit, Lester Brown of the Worldwatch Institute adds:

> Glowing economic reports are possible even as the economic policies that generate them are destroying the resource base.....no business would be run along those lines, yet national governments proceed blithely on the basis of monthly figures of aggregate growth, with no systematic analysis as to whether that growth has come from greater employment, from greater utilisation of capital assets, from increased use of natural resources or from greater productivity... resource indicators should include all natural and human resources.

An Adjusted National Product (ANP) is proposed by Christian Leipert, a new economist working in Berlin. It includes what he calls 'defensive expenditure', the external costs of the general growth process: for example the costs of environmental protection.

Should growth be banned? The compilers of *The Living Economy* argue that the equation *growth equals welfare* is invalid because three vital questions are left unanswered: growth for what? growth for whom? and growth with what side-effects? The authors argue that growth can only be regarded as positive if it has taken place through the production of goods and services that are inherently valuable and beneficial, that have been distributed widely through society and whose benefits outweigh their detrimental effects. Further, the pursuit of growth is actually likely to intensify the very economic problems which it is means to solve, chief among them inflation and unemployment.

Ridiculing the notion of unstoppable growth, the

Brazilian agronomist, Jose Lutzenberger, uses the language of cybernetics to suggest that we are introducing an element of positive feedback, or exponential behaviour into the system.

> Exponential behaviour is the type you see in a snowball. The snowball receives positive feedback; as it rolls, it becomes bigger because more snow sticks to it, and as it grows, it rolls faster and so on. But this kind of behaviour is inherently unstable. It is impossible to keep the snowball rolling eternally: there is not enough slope or snow for it in the whole world. Anyway, long before it can become too big it disintegrates and forms a tremendous avalanche. This is exactly what is happening today, as long as we keep introducing positive feedback into our economies. We are already reaching the point of avalanche...We must go for another type of behaviour—not exponential but homeostatic. (8)

Ivan Illich, the brilliant iconaclastic priest turned political activist, has been attacking capitalism on its soft underbelly for years. He suggests that the right economy would be somewhere in between the growth-oriented ones we have today and their theoretical opposite, which he discerns in "a great variety of societies where existence is organised around subsistence activities, each community choosing its unique lifestyle tempered by scepticism about the claims of growth". (9)

Outright 'steady-staters' who reject all growth are in a minority among the new economists. One of these, Professor Herman Daly of Louisiana University, proposes to get from what he calls 'growthmania' to the steady-state economy by limiting excessive production and extraction through taxation, and restricting inequalities of income so that nobody earns more than ten times as much as anybody else. Summing up the wholistic approach, James Robertson predicts that, "the new name of the game will be to do with human growth in a social, ecological and spiritual perspective and that religion, politics, and economics will be together again in this new vision of the meaning of life". (10)

A BASIC INCOME FOR ALL

The most ambitious scheme of the new economics is also the most controversial: a Basic Income (BI) or national wage for everyone, whether they work or not. Industrial society already pays the equivalent of a basic income—but does so through dole and benefit payments that are unwieldy, expensive to operate, humiliating to the recipient and stifling of initiative because they include a disincentive from working. BI would be paid to every man, woman and child as of right and with no questions asked. The scheme would be financed, first, by the administrative saving involved (BI could be paid out by computerised giro); secondly, by the higher rate of tax that employers could pay when they are liberated from social security payments and other burdens on their labour force.

Under the system, employers would enjoy greater flexibility in the use of labour; they could take on more part-time and short-contract staff. This would help industry to modernise, become more profitable and thus pay higher taxes. Some advocates of BI expect wages to be lower, because workers already receiving the minumum wage would need less.

The immediate aim is to eliminate the 'poverty trap' imposed by the dole and benefit system in conditions of high unemployment. At present, in Britain and elsewhere, it often makes no economic sense to work, as Professor Charles Handy of the London Business School observes:

If you are on unemployment benefit and you earn more than £2 a day venturing into self-employment (which is what everybody should do) it becomes a crime—unless you declare it. But if you declare it, it becomes a 100% marginal rate of taxation. In other words, it is deducted from your benefit. This is no way to encourage people to take care of themselves, to become self-reliant and responsible. (11)

The ultimate aim of BI goes further. James Robertson, another supporter, considers it could "facilitate a change of direction to a new work order". In a free labour market, people could work as much or as little as they wished.

Would we become lazy if we no longer had to work? The new economists have a different reading of character, arguing that people would be liberated to lead more active and socially useful lives. Women, in particular, would be freed from their subservient economic role; the stereotyped role-playing of the nuclear family could be abolished in a regime in which both men and women would be free to work, or study, or do voluntary work. State pensions could be abolished and people could retire when they pleased. In all, people would probably do more work, not less. James Robertson considered that such a scheme would start reversing the process that began several hundred years ago, when the common people, deprived of access to land through the enclosures of the 18th and 19th centuries, could no longer feed themselves and so became dependant upon waged labour.

The idea of a 'tax credit' or social dividend was mooted in Britain in the 1920s and was later taken up in the United States by Milton Friedman, reappearing in amended form as negative income tax. In times of prosperity and full employment, the idea of BI lost relevance, but interest has now reawakened. In Britain, costed proposals were submitted to a House of Commons committee inquiry in 1982. A feasibility study was recommended and later undertaken by the Basic Income Research Group (BIRG), sponsored by the National Council of Voluntary Organisations, an organisation not linked to the new economics. BIRG points out that BI combines the compassion of the welfare state with the efficiency of the free market. Since it could be operated by computer and paid into personal giro accounts, nobody need queue.

> Everyone receives at least a basic subsistence already; few starve. All that would be changed is the route by which the money is distributed. Nor need there be any net increase in personal taxation. The average family would pay somewhat more in actual tax, partly due to the removal of personal and marriage allowences and mortage interest relief, but all its members, young and old, male and female, would receive a basic income to balance this.(12)

How much would BI cost? Hermione Parker, a supporter of the scheme, concluded after a detailed costing for BIRG that a full-blown BI scheme without any means tested benefits, "would be extremely expensive and would almost certainly fail to achieve the main objective, which is the prevention of poverty". She concluded that the best solution was a "judicious combination of both universality (basic income or social dividend) and selectivity (negative income tax)".

The Institute for Fiscal Studies opposes the BI scheme, both on the grounds of principle and of expense. But Hermione Parker pointed out that this Institute, firmly anchored to prevailing structures, continued to work on the outdated basis of wives and children as dependents of the 'male breadwinner'.

The still unsolved dilemma is that a fully-fledged basic income scheme might push tax rates too high, thereby defeating some of the scheme's economic objectives, while a partial scheme might reintroduce much of the bureaucracy that BI seeks to eliminate, while not providing a high enough income for meaningful independence. Schumacher opposed similar schemes because they would increase dependency and inflate the importance of the state. Any BI scheme would have to be national and would therefore work against semi-autonomous, decentralised communities.

However, the scheme now has supporters even outside the new economics movement. One of these is Peter Ashby, who worked as head of the National Council for Voluntary Organizations policy planning unit during its BI research programme. Unlike the new economists, Ashby envisages BI in the context of growth and full employment. He told us he thought a fully-fledged scheme was, "not on the agenda this century: it would imply a basic income tax rate of 70p to 80p in the pound". Ashby favours a partial scheme, conceding that the basic income would need to be topped up through employment. He insists that whatever the level of payment the scheme must be universal and unconditional; "a conditional basic income scheme would serve to increase the state's power, while an unconditional scheme would increase the rights of individuals".

Again unlike the new economists, Ashby does not concede that basic income must lead to lower wages. "You have to remember that BI doesn't represent new money: it is existing social security benefits, tax reliefs and allowances recycled to provide a unified system of income maintainance. These payments do not of themselves increase workers' income from the state and therefore it would be unrealistic to expect wages to fall".

GREEN MONEY, GREEN INVESTMENT

Can we invest our savings in a sustainable economy, and escape from the tyranny of money? When we put our money into facelesss institutions like building societies or the Stock Exchange, we risk supporting activities we disapprove of, from the manufacture of chemical fertilisers to the building of nuclear power stations. Ethical investment companies have been started and there are also local currency schemes, devised to run parallel with national currencies but designed to benefit local communities.

Local currencies, or 'green dollars', have worked successfully in the USA and Canada, and several are at the planning stage in Europe. A successful scheme in British Columbia, operating since 1983, handled some $250,000 worth of green dollar trade in its first twenty months. This is called a LETS (local exchange trading system).

The LETS system is described by Landsman (Community Services Ltd), in the TOES survey, as a self-regulating economic network which allows its members to issue and manage their own money supply within a bounded system.The LETS scheme in Courtney, British Columbia, began as a small barter club where people found it hard to match up each other's offers and requirements. The next step was a notice board advertising needs and offers of services and goods. After that, accounts began to be kept in an internal money unit. Trading volume reachd $300,000 in three years. Michael Linton, who set the scheme up, said these dollars, unlike those issued by the Bank of Canada, were, "just entries in a book of accounts. So some people have some green dollars to their name and other people have a negative account of green dollars because they have spent some before they've earned it back". Linton explained:

> Every dollar in the LETS system is backed by somebody's promise. That actually makes it the strongest currency in existence, principally because the person who makes the promise is always going to be able to redeem it. That is to say, he's around in the community and he cannot fail to earn it back—if he's willing to do something—anything. . . He could say I'm available to mow your lawn for green dollars, look after your kids, consult in your business. . . If it's something someone conceivably wants. . . they'll buy it. . . People will fulfill their own promises when the facility

for them to do so is there, and that's the key distinction. With conventional money, people make promises and you can't believe a word of it.(13)

The LETS scheme or any variation has three community advantages; local 'money' is kept within the community with greater local control of the local economy; speculation is prevented because green dollars have only local value and finally there is a free flow of those in the community who have goods and services to offer. Local currency schemes are still experimental, yet they provide a simple but effective means to encourage local economic activity and reactivate communities that have become impoverished.

Hazel Henderson has told of a scheme called a *service credit system*, operating in her home State of Florida. She compared it to, "an official blood bank, crediting volunteers with work they do in the community, so that eventually we hope we can give out what we call service credit cards, which would enable volunteers in good standing in the community who've racked up so many hours to have a little plastic credit card with their name on it". In every place she visited, people were, "inventing either alternative limited purpose currencies, or they are growing a home-grown information economy when they're linking needs and recources, exchanging skills, doing learning networks, many of them using personal computers. And they're doubling up in houses and figuring out all kinds of mutual aid and barter schemes." (14)

Investment in ecologically sound ventures is an aspect of new economics that has got well beyond the drawing board. The Mercury Provident Society enables its investors to lend on favourable terms to enterprises conceived 'for the good of society'. The Friends Provident Society has launched the Stewardship Fund, a unit trust enabling investors to back selected responsible public companies.

In the United States more than $50 billion have been channelled through institutions operating under the umbrella of 'socially responsible investment'. Calvert Social Investment, for example, involves managers active in labour relations, targeted pension investment, civil liberties and energy conservation. Many companies have been listed in a report by Giles Chitty, a former New York finance manager whose British venture, the Financial Initiative, was founded in 1984.

The Financial Initiative, the most successful British venture in its field, seeks to match investors wishing to support and profit from enterprises, 'meeting human and ecological standards and conceived for the good of the whole'. The company supports activities which, 'encourage human growth, participation and reponsibility; help conserve a sustainable ecological environment; build co-operation and peace rather than fuel destructive competition and conflict; promote human health—physical, mental and spiritual'. Projects financed by the company include whole food producers and alternative energy plants. The firm has branched out into portfolio management and helped found the Ethical Investment Fund.

NEW ECONOMICS AND OLD

An adoption of the new economic ideas would mean that economic life as we know it would be totally altered. Therefore no early rapprochement can be expected. However, more and more official economists are getting some of the message. David Pearce of University College London took part in a TOES meeting and set out the arguments for ecological economics in his inaugural lecture as Professor of Economics in 1985. He spoke of 'rules' that had been established by environmental economics: that no renewable resources should be harvested at a rate which exceeds the sustainable yield; that we should not discard waste into the environment at a rate which exceeds its ability to degrade that waste; and that the assimilative capacity of the natural environment must be managed as a renewable resource.

A liberal critique of the new economics was given by Christopher Huhne, *The Guardian's* economics editor, before the 1985 TOES meeting. Huhne wrote: "kernels of truth in the green argument could get lost where they may count, because of the profoundly wrong fallacies, so it is worth separating the wheat from the chaff". Dismissing apprehensions about growth in a finite world, Huhne wrote that the Club of Rome's warnings had ignored the fact that scarcity leads to price rises which leads to a fall in demand— which is what happened during the first oil crisis. Problem solved, Huhne says—apart from the incovenience of sharp price fluctuations and the fact that oil will, after all, run out one day. Huhne admits that ecologists have a point in asking for resources to be counted. "A change in accounting conventions would be useful if only in highlighting our need to maintain our natural and man-made capital." He adds that "some sort of Quality of Life Index, such as the Japanese have, would be a valuable supplement to GDP or NNP (Net National Product)".

But for Huhne, "it seems to beggar belief that the indicators of welfare, which have improved in line with the growth of national income, do not signify material gains: lives themselves, after all, are longer on average by 15 years than they were at the turn of the century; 86% had holidays of four weeks or more in 1981 compared with only 7% in 1970; hours of work had fallen from 47 a week in 1970 to 44 by 1981. We have more phones, cars, and disposable incomes, all of them increasing choice and hence individual freedom." He goes on to his 'bottom line' argument that people in democracies have consistently chosen governments bent on the same course.

Huhne concludes that slower growth could only postpone the effects of pollution; that the best hope lies in a substantial investment in non-fossil fuel, "and that in turn requires an increase in GDP - and even in Net National Product. Let us by all means have 'green' growth - but plenty of it. Economic stagnation will solve nobody's problems."(15)

Here was the old economics trying, at least, to be fair. The counter arguments would point out that the predictable fall in oil prices will not prevent their equally predictable rise in a few more years, followed by a new oil crisis. In addition, while many people may be working shorter hours as a result of growth, almost as many, after centuries of expansion now work no hours at all. For the employed, longer paid holidays may compensate for the tension, alienation and stress of living in industrial society. Would people living wholistically and convivially, sustained by *ownwork* and Basic Income, need holidays at all? Besides, if more and more people enjoy 'choice and individual freedom' by driving more and more cars on more and more holidays, where will be the motorways wide enough to accomodate them? And, anyway, where on earth will they go?

Notes:

(1)   Erich Fromm, *To Have or To Be*, page 15.

(2)   ibid, page 16.

(3)   Hazel Henderson, *The Politics of the Solar Age*.

(4)   Ekins, *The Living Economy*, pages 98-99.

(5)   Schumacher, *Good Work*, page 57.

(6)   Schumacher, *Good Work*, page 19.

(7)   Hazel Henderson, *The Politics of the Solar Age*, page 292.

(8)   Inglis, *The New Economic Agenda*, page 162.

(9)   Ivan Illich, *Shadow Work*.

(10) James Robertson, *The Sane Alternative*.

(11) Inglis, op. cit, page 46.

(12) Keith Roberts, *BIRG Bulletin Spring 1985*.

(13) Interviewed on CBC : *New Ideas on Ecology and Economics, 1986*.

(14) Interviewed on CBC : *New Ideas on Ecology and Economics, 1986*.

(15) Christopher Huhne, *The Guardian, 1986*.

CHAPTER FOUR

Ownwork

Manchester Cold Rollers Ltd: Six of the nine man Co-operative, Denis Thorpe, The Guardian

Ownwork

INDUSTRIAL society has given us material comforts and personal freedom for many, but it has distorted and impoverished two basic aspects of living—our work and our communities. Can the balance of profit and loss be measured? In pre-industrial times almost everyone worked at or near home and home was part of a community in which living may have been harsh, but which formed a supportive web of mutual contacts, rights and obligations. The life of industrial man is rigidly segregated and work is something done away from home and unrelated to domestic life. The separation impoverishes both. In leaving his home to go to work—he also leaves his community. The result is that instead of communities, he has blocks of flats and rows of council houses or, if he is luckier, suburbs, dormitory towns and villages in which he lives behind walls and hedges. Industrial woman, who joined the work force in large numbers only this century, follows the same alienating pattern with the additional burden of continuing her traditional role as housewife.

The social historian, Peter Lasslett, assessed the gains and losses of the world we have lost through industrialisation. Looking at the family of a London master baker in the year

1619, in which old people, distant relatives and apprentices swelled the hardworking household, he noted that everyone had a role which was, 'emotionally highly symbolic and highly satisfying':

> We may feel that in a whole society organised like this, in spite of all the subordination, the exploitation and the obliteration of those who were young, or feminine, or in service, everyone belonged in a group, a family group. Everyone had his circle of affection: every relationship could be seen as a love relationship.(1)

Today, we pay a heavy price for the benefits of our mass societies: in increased amounts of stress, loneliness and emotional starvation. Can we get back to the conviviality and dense human relations of real work, real homes and real communities without bringing back the hardships and injustices? The time seems propitious. The great manufacturing industries which sucked whole populations into the towns are now being shut down or modernised, making a large labour force redundant. This provides an opportunity for fundamental change. If full-time jobs are no longer going to be available for everyone or even most people throughout their working lives, we can surely think of better ways to pass the time than the enforced and costly idleness of the dole.

In the countryside, too, new opportunities are arising as the crisis in agriculture bites harder. The food mountains pile up and the levels of pollution and environmental damage may soon become intolerable. Are there viable solutions for repopulating rural areas, enabling people once more to grow some of their own food instead of having to buy processed food at supermarkets?

We are not talking about a dream of an alternative society in the minds of a few visionaries. In town and country the new society is breaking through, because the old is breaking down. "Unemployed people are in effect pioneering a new way of living; they have nothing to lose so they can find the way forward, and we have to learn from them", we were told in Teesside, Northern Britain, by John Wilcox, an industrial chaplain. At Middlesborough, he had helped conduct an informal survey of two groups—one employed at the nearby steelworks, the other unemployed.

> The unemployed were more hopeful. The point is they had gone through the trough of despond and come out the other side. Richness is not linked to money but to activities. The people at work spoke of insecurities, the pressures they faced, the stress and pollution of their lives. Of course the unemployed said they would take a job if offered, citing mainly the feeling of guilt through not 'working' officially. A new creativity must be allowed to blossom and develop.

Creativity has appeared in various urban and rural initiatives. Theoretical guidelines, if any are needed, have been laid down in the Schumacher tradition by a succession of writers. The aim is to reintegrate work with private life and this means escaping from the identitification of work with employment. Why should we work? Schumacher suggested three reasons:

> First, to provide necessary and useful goods and services; second, to enable everyone of us to use and thereby perfect our gifts like good stewards; third, to do so in service to, and in co-operation with others, so as to liberate ourselves from our inborn egocentricity. (2)

James Robertson's useful concept of *ownwork* suits the conditions of our post-industrial age.

> *Ownwork* means activity which is purposeful and important, and which people organise and control for themselves. It may be either paid or unpaid. It is done by people as individuals

or as household members; it is done by groups of people working together; and it is done by people who live in a particular locality, working locally to meet local needs...Just as the Lutheran ethic taught that worldly work was more real than withdrawal into the artificial, abstracted sphere of ecclesiastical life, so the new work ethic now will teach that to immerse oneself in today's organisational world is to sink into a world of abstractions and turn one's back on real life; and that real life means real experience, and real work means finding ways of acting directly to meet needs—one's own, other peoples' and, increasingly, the survival needs of the natural world which supports us. (3)

How could we divide time between ownwork, paid work, study and our other activities? Charles Handy calculates that until recently, people in industrial societies worked one hundred and two thousand hours a year: forty-seven hours a week, for forty-seven weeks, for forty-seven years. Today, since few people get into the system before the age of twenty and many leave in their fifties, this has been reduced to fifty thousand: thirty-five hours a week, for forty-five weeks, for thirty-two years. Handy suggests that this fifty thousand norm should be spent in an 'á-la-carte' way to suit individual tastes.

Ownwork should not be confused with housework. Industrial societies have used this woman's work as an unpaid and unacknowledged, though essential prop to the system. Ivan Illich calls this shadow work, insisting it has nothing to do with the subsistence work of pre-industrial societies. He has identified shadow work as, "the unpaid complement of industrial labour and services. A kind of forced labour or industrial serfdom in the service of commodity-intensive economics must be carefully distinguished from subsistence-orientated work lying outside the industrial system". In place of this arrangement, Illich recommends its opposite, which, "prevails when a community chooses a subsistence-orientated way of life":

> There, the inversion of development, the replacement of
> consumer goods by personal action, of industrial tools by
> convivial tools is the goal...There, the guitar is valued over
> the record, the library over the schoolroom, the backyard
> garden over the supermarket selection. There the personal
> control of each worker over his means of production
> determines the small horizon of each enterprise, a horizon
> which is a necessary condition for social production and the
> unfolding of each worker's individuality. This mode of
> production also exists in slavery, serfdom and other forms of
> dependence. But it flourishes, releases energy, acquires its
> adequate and classical form only where the worker is the free
> owner of his tools and resources; only then can the artisan
> perform like a virtuoso. This mode of production can be
> maintained only within the limits that nature dictates to both
> production and society. There, useful unemployment is
> valued while wage labour, within limits, is merely
> tolerated.(4)

OWNWORK AND SOCIALISM

A transition from jobbed work to ownwork will not be
without problems, for as long as the former dominates and
commands the higher standard of living, the latter will be at a
disadvantage and open to exploitation. Trade unions are
worried about this too and are largely hostile to the new
economics as a result. A senior official of the Trades Union
Congress, David Lea, told us that, "the movement for
ownwork carries the danger of an unholy alliance between
people who don't want full employment in order to keep
workers and unions in a weak position, and those who want to
go back to some sort of agrarian society". (5)

Ivan Illich also warned that, "unpaid work guided by

professionals could spread through a repressive, ecological welfare society. Women's serfdom in the domestic sphere is the most obvious example today." (6)

We have already seen that the traditional Left, still wedded to growth and the illusion of full employment, has little time for the new economics. However, some Socialists have realised that since traditional work is disappearing in any case, new patterns of work must evolve. André Gortz, the leading French writer in this field, finds the working class divided in three separate strands: tenured workers; the unemployed; and the 'non-class of non-workers', who are both deskilled and alienated from work. Gortz warns that one scenario for the future is an aggressive, authoritarian, state-regulated capitalism (in Britain many feel this has already arrived). He advocates instead, "a post-industrial society in which jobbed work will be equitably shared out and peoples' major occupation may be one or a number of self-defined activities, carried out not for money but for the interest, pleasure or benefit incurred". (7)

In Britain many people on the Left have followed a similar line. We shall describe in a later chapter how Mike Cooley, who was a leader of the Lucas Airospace adventure, became a trade unionist of the post-industrial school. In that newer tradition, John Keane and John Owens urge Socialists to demonstrate that, "a new ideal is needed to replace the undesirable and the unrepeatable, and therefore obsolete, ideal of full male employment". These writers argue that Socialists must, "invent viable strategies for ending the tyranny of paid work, thereby making possible a post-employment society which maximises individuals' choice of whether, or how much, they work for pay".(8)

Work-sharing has emerged in the established Left as a popular remedy for unemployment. However, without more radical changes towards new patterns of working, it cannot make much headway. There is resistance from trade unionists, who see it as a recipe for lower wages; from

Socialists, who still think full employment is possible and therefore consider work-sharing defeatist and from people at work, who feel that they cannot 'afford' lower pay because of their lifestyle, their cars, holidays and mortgages. Work-sharing can only become widespread as part of broader change—the move to the a-la-carte attitude to work advocated by James Robertson and Charles Handy. People will have to rethink their priorities.

Many have already done so. Guy Dauncey, whom we met in chapter two, told us he found work-sharing becoming more popular in the USA and Canada:

> At least 30% of people want to do less work for less money. In USA, there is a whole network of voluntary work options. A resource centre set up on Vancouver Island in British Columbia, by the Canadian Association of Mental Health, noticed half their clients coming in stressed out because they had no work, the other half stressed out because they had too much work! There is a whole panoply of measures: deferred salary, leave pans, voluntary time. All of them might be found in a single scheme: you can save up part of your income to pay for a year off, with guaranteed job back after your sabbatical. You need a mixture: flexible ways of working for less pay.

Additional impetus for flexible work patterns comes from industry. Many large firms are finding they can reduce labour costs by employing people on short contracts, or part-time; or else 'hive off' their skilled workers and help them to form their own mini-business, which then supplies the parent-firm on contract. At worst, this trend can open the way to exploitation reminiscent of old-style cottage-industries. At best, it opens the way to the new society, especially if some form of Basic Income is introduced along the lines we explored in chapter three.

Flexi-time and shared work are particularly attractive to

women with families, who want to spend time with young children, but who also need the money and interest that a job provides.

WORKING IN THE COUNTRY

Ownwork cannot flourish in cities alone. For decades city dwellers in industrial countries have been moving out to rural areas and this trend will accelerate as a new work and community ethic begins to prevail. In Britain and elsewhere, the trend is being blocked by a combination of high land prices and restrictive planning regulations. Our Town and Country Planning Acts were originally designed to protect the countryside. Now they have often out-lived their usefulness and exist as shields for the amenities of privileged middle class rural inhabitants. Rural areas are also kept artificially empty of people for the sake of industrial farming that employs virtually nobody and produces unwanted surpluses at huge cost.

Meanwhile people stay trapped, unproductive and miserable in cities which no longer need them. One solution is to repopulate the villages, putting unused energy to work by letting people grow some, at least, of their own food. Mixed, family farming happens to be the most productive as well as the most ecological use of land. Land prices are still too high in most industrial countries to allow people to recreate many family farms, but small-holdings, less costly to buy, can be organically run on economically sound and environmentally rewarding lines. However, until amenities like schools and bus services, local shops and village halls are returned or reopened in the countryside, the quality of life is too bleak to encourage any but the most dedicated.

An experiment in repopulating the British countryside is the Lightmoor co-operative, near Telford New Town in Shropshire. Families have been building this twenty-two acre village, where they plan to live from paid work for half of their time and devote the rest to smallholdings and community life. The fourteen families at Lightmoor form a majority in a non-profit-making company which also includes representatives of the County Council and the more than usually enlightened local Development Corporation. The village company was allocated the land, first on lease, later as freehold and the company in turn offered sub-leases to each household. The scheme was set up by Tony Gibson, a writer, who aims to reform the theory and practice of rural planning. Gibson told us he saw the rural neighbourhood of the future as made up of, "a few small clusters of houses, workshops and market gardens, with open country and woodland in between".

Lightmoor is a working neighbourhood—not just dwellings but also livelihoods. It is for people who value a certain degree of independence and privacy but also want to help each other out. The same idea could easily work in an exhausted pithead, in a dockland, a devastated inner-city area, or in neglected areas of one-time farmland. A community like this needs to apply appropriate technology, and Lightmoor is high-tech plus low-tech. A computer in the kitchen, a pig in the back yard. Some Lightmoor members will in fact be computer programming; some will continue to work outside in their present jobs and others will work partly inside and partly out. We're setting up a small workshop. There is a teacher of Art & Design who has built his workshop and hopes eventually to be producing furniture and fitted kitchens. There's a woman who's going to be a caterer, and a mechanic. Nearly everybody wants to raise a bit of food.

ART FOR EVERYONE

Lightmoor provides an excellent template for similar

schemes.

Ownwork will change our conception of time and the way we divide up our days. Most of the present rigid divisions will disappear. There will be time to play and to create. When the shift to a more wholistic style of life becomes more widespread, one of the most exhilarating developments will be the part that art will play in everyone's life. By art we mean, not a narrow interpretation of pictures seen in a gallery, programmes watched on television or costly performances of 19th century operas. We mean all the performing and creative arts and the artefacts, pots, chairs, rugs which people create for themselves.

Art can be used as a metaphor for society. Our arts reflect our involvement with, or our alienation from, the world around us. Much of the 'art' surrounding us today is mediocre, trivial and dull. In primitive societies art, everyday life and religion are so intertwined that there is little separation. Music, dance, pottery, carving and weaving are accessible to and created by everyone. Specialists like the shaman, the witchdoctor, the blacksmith, exist but they are not so separated from the community, nor is their art incomprehensible to most people, like that of the practitioners of High Art in our societies.

In Western society during the last few centuries, art has grown increasingly estranged from people, a development which has accelerated in the last hundred years. For many of us, art has become less an expression of our joy of life or our experience of the sacred, than the mere expression of group identity, or a status symbol.

During the Renaissance, the artist as individual made his appearance. The individual artist reached heights of sublimity that have rarely been equalled either before or since. Michaelangelo seemed almost to create on a par with God. But this individualism degenerated into the pretentious and the trivial as Western society became increasingly industrialised. Geniuses still existed, they still do, but their work is no longer accessible, except to an educated élite. In Shakespeare's time any Londoner visiting The Globe theatre would have laughed at his jokes or at Ben Jonson's. A typical Londoner today would be unlikely to visit the Tate Gallery or enjoy a Schoenberg symphony. Art has now bifurcated into High Art and entertainment and in both cases it is generally produced for us, not by us. Entertainment has become a commodity that we are encouraged to buy. The rules of the market apply—a quick profit and a planned obsolescence so that we purchase again as soon as possible.

It is debatable how much art was enjoyed by the majority of people in previous eras. We would argue that spectacles in which the audience participated were available and appreciated far more than they are in industrial society. Art of this kind survives only in countries considered less advanced. In our own societies people once took part in creative activities in a way that we no longer do. The great cathedrals were community projects; the festivals to mark the passage of the year were communal activities with spiritual as well as temporal meaning; the durable artefacts that people used were self-made or produced by craftsmen.

The growth of mass production spelled the death of the craftsman and the need for a docile force of factory workers, aware of the clock, spelled the death of the festivals. However, festivals and folk art, relics of a pagan past, have survived, often in attentuated or degenerate forms, despite official disapproval.

Folk art, by which we mean the participation of many people, not just professional specialists, has survived in non-industrial parts of the world. It can still be seen—if you hurry. Housewives in Botswana decorate their mud houses; Indian women paint original designs with henna on their feet and hands; in Bali musicians play the gamelin, composing each piece afresh, because they don't write down the music. These art forms, like the societies which produce them, are fragile in face of attack by technological society with its insistence on the bought and paid for.

There are signs, however, that people are beginning once more to appreciate folk art, both for its beauty and the enhancement it brings to daily life. Now is the time for a revival. For the moment, the split between high and low art remains; few of us can afford a seat at the opera, or a high-quality art book costing £30. At the grassroots level, the situation looks more promising and is certainly more fun. In Britain—a multi-cultural country despite itself—ethnic minorites begin to explore their cultural identities through different art forms. For the last few years, West Indians in London's Notting Hill Gate district have held an annual carnival. Street festivals and street parties in inner-city areas are growing in numbers and popularity. While the rock and pop scene remains heavily commercialised, thousands of young people dance and make music together.

Both in Europe and the United States, the lost art of storytelling is being revived. While she was taking part in the second International Storytellers' Festival in London, Diane Wolkstein remarked:

> The colder we become, the more mechanical, the more
> computerised, the greater the need in the human psyche.
> Storytelling is the opposite of television; the tales are
> elemental and deal with conflicts and changes in life. (9)

Ritual and art are recombining. In America the interest in Native American culture ties in with the growing ecological awareness of the bio-regional movement. There are also attempts to recreate some ancient British festivals, but these have not caught popular imagination to any appreciable extent. There is a slightly forced quality of protesting too much about dancing round the maypole or celebrating the winter solstice, but their appeal is widening. In the summer of 1986, a convoy of travellers tried to celebrate the summer solstice at Stonehenge in Wiltshire.

They were prevented. Even when the convoy tried to camp on common land they were opposed with irrational hatred by local people with the support of the authorities. The event showed how difficult it is to break out of the conventional mould; yet there was considerable public sympathy for the travellers.

John Seymour, one of the leading Britsh exponents of a wholistic way of life, has written of the growing interest in craftwork. "I believe that as more and more craftspeople fight through, in town as well as country, something like the old community interrelationships will awaken and grow again."(10) Seymour's vision of an arty-crafty, folksy world can easily be poked fun at. But why not ridicule the glitzy, artifical world of telly culture? Anything new, or a restoration of anything old, appears at first sight bizarre, archaic, or ridiculous. But there is a simple test to discover whether you agree with Seymour about the value of the hand-crafted object. Hold two bowls in your hands, one of plastic, one of wood; which pleases you more?

Notes:
(1)   Peter Laslett, *The World We Have Lost*.
(2)   E.F. Schumacher, *Good Work*, page 3.
(3)   James Robertson, *Future Work*, page 69.
(4)   Ivan Illich, *Shadow Work*, page 13.
(5)   Interview with David Lea, Assistant General Secretary of TUC, in 1984.
(6)   Ivan Illich, *Shadow Work*, page 17.
(7)   Andr Gortz, *Paths to Paradise*.
(8)   John Keane and John Owens, *After Full Employment*, page 178.
(9)   *The Guardian*, January 19, 1987.
(10) John Seymour, *The Forgotten Arts*, page 32.

CHAPTER FIVE

Decolonised Communities

Working from the Bottom Up, The Lightmoor Community
Tony Gibson, Lightmoor Project

Decolonised Communities

IN GLASGOW'S run-down suburb of Easterhouse, seventy per cent of the population of fifty thousand lives off the dole. This model dormitory estate for workers was built in the 1930s. Today, Easterhouse has a dozen betting shops, but no cinema or restaurant and hardly any pubs. In 1978, Chris Elphic, a young social worker, and some friends organised a group to stage an Arts festival. When it was over, the group decided to go on celebrating—and they never stopped. They founded the Easterhouse Festival Society, which held meetings, put on plays, pantomimes and arts shows. The Society branched out and helped people turn hobbies like puppet-making and carpentry into part-time jobs. Before long it was in the business of organising regular jobs. The Festival, as it came to be called, became famous as a symbol of the grassroots economy.

The Society retained its festive name because of its conviction that talent and conviviality were more immediately needed even than jobs. The Festival turned a derelict plot into a playground and a row of shops and then organised local artists to surround it with a mural mosaic, depicting peace and ecological harmony. The mosaic, two hundred and forty feet long and six feet high, is the largest in

Britain and one of Scotland's most distinguished works of urban art. The Festival later attracted regional grants to found an industrial holding company that let out work space and provided management help for small business ventures.

Easterhouse has had its counterparts in scores of towns and many rural areas, where people on the dole have found activity outside conventional employment. These groups have been helped by government and local agencies, firms and foundations, churches and volunteers. The business of getting the unemployed 'off the streets' has generated a new sense of community. A disparate, ad-hoc alliance has arisen of unemployed people and their helpers, to set up community businesses, resource centres, workspaces or drop-in centres.

At Easterhouse in 1985, we found a satisfied customer of the grassroots economy in James Riley, who had just started his own contracting firm. He had been on the dole for a year. "There was nothing left at Easterhouse: nothing to do, people didn't even know their neighbours. I was going to leave, when I heard about the Festival." The society put up the £1,000 capital guarantee Riley needed to qualify for a national Enterprise Allowance grant.

In Govan, a run-down suburb of Glasgow, we talked to Linda Ecklin, another grassroots entrepreneur. She had borrowed an empty shop for a fortnight in her home town of Saltcoats, to hold a jumble sale. That developed into a community second-hand business and then Linda was running a knitting ring. She moved to Govan where she got an Urban Aid grant to start a larger home-knitting ring. She was working with sixty people, using her own designs and working to order, in an old school converted into workspaces by Strathclyde Community Business. When we met her, she was planning to help other young Govanites out of their post-industrial apathy by running a cafe started by a church group.

John Pierce, who ran the community business in which Linda Echlin had her office, got his money from the Scottish Development Agency. But he told us he is often at odds with the SDA: "They think of conventional recovery, full employment and all that. We think of something new."

In Walsall, in the Midlands, where unemployment has reached 80%, a group of people on the dole founded the Pleck Community Association in 1982. At first, they received funds from the Manpower Service Commission's Community Programme to start an unemployment day centre offering advice, work experience and recreation. The Association later took over a milk round, a fish and chip van and formed a group of co-operatives in knitwear, building, plumbing and car component recycling. Regeneration produced in this way helped persuade the central government to grant urban aid money to the area. (1)

In Britain the necessary cash for these local projects often comes from the Manpower Services Commission (MSC). The money is received with misgivings because many people in the business of helping the unemployed see the MSC as a cosmetic body designed to keep unemployment statistics down and young people off the streets. But they take the money all the same. There is a creative irony in a situation where authority is working so closely with people trying to establish a different society. Some of the people closely involved in negotiating government initiatives are visionaries, like Guy Dauncey, who teaches people to use the system. But he dreams of a different society.

Others are more down to earth, like Colin Ball, Director of the Centre for Employment Initiatives in London. His research and consultancy firm, in London and the provinces, helps local government agencies and private firms give creative aid to the unemployed. Ball identifies two extremes in the grassroots economy:

At one end, the here-and-now people: these offer the

palliatives, temporary jobs—things the MSC offers. At the other end, the 'hello sky, hello trees' brigade: that includes the new economics, Harford Thomas in *The Guardian* and that mystic Guy Dauncey. There is a wide spectrum in between—people who think we must do something now, in a thoroughly practical way, that is more than a palliative. We need that bridging ground between the extremes; we need a whole range of projects—a supermarket approach. [Interview with the authors].

So varied are these initiatives that a service is needed to keep people in touch. In Glasgow, the Local Economic Development Information Service (LEDIS) stores and distributes information sheets on hundreds of projects to firms, local governments and private subscribers.

Eventually, these disparate new mini-communities will need to be linked in a computer network. Pioneer networks are already at work. One of these, UNET, links initiatives and community groups working alongside the unemployed. UNET is the successor of the British Unemployment Resources Network, which was set up in 1980 by the Birmingham Settlement to encourage self-help among the unemployed by linking them in a network. At the end of 1986, UNET was offering electronic mail and information on management and consultancy to the twenty groups it had 'on line'.

A new society may be breaking through in these urban initiatives, but the way is uphill all the same. Unlike medieval monasteries or Israeli kibbutzim, these ventures operate outside and potentially in opposition to, the prevailing culture. As we have seen, they have to go begging for grants. A Basic Income Scheme of the kind envisaged by the new economists, which we described in chapter three, would solve the problem of resources, but that is not on any immediate agenda.

We talked to Chris Elphic, co-founder of the Easterhouse Festival Society, in 1986, eighteen months after our first visit. Many problems had surfaced on the local and national levels. Funds from the Government's Urban Project had run out after seven years and not been renewed. The Strathclyde Region had taken back its office space, forcing the Society to use its industrial holding company as a base and to dismiss its permanent staff of eight, including Elphic. The Festival was now continuing with a reduced staff and private funds, including money from ethical investment groups in Britain and the USA. The society had found it difficult to co-exist with authority. Chris Elphic is saddened, though not discouraged:

> In the long run the politicians and officials could not handle our independence. Nor could they take the way we mixed up arts and employment: they couldn't fit the two together the way we did. We had the option to pack up or be taken over and we refused both. Partnership with the private sector is the only way forward in the long run. Our experience shows we need a vibrant voluntary sector alongside the statutory sector. It's difficult for people to appreciate the effects of poverty in a place like Easterhouse. Drug abuse has got much worse: the family is breaking down. People like the Festival Society represent a small minority: the drug culture is much more dominant than we are. Community efforts to improve the quality of life is being sabotaged. We used to get young people deliberately sent to sabotage meetings: the police know about it: it's the drug dealers who organise that against us. The police have their work cut out just containing thugs. People like Guy Dauncey paint too rosy a picture. Marginal areas like Easterhouse are getting bigger and bigger, more and more. Larger areas are getting less and less affluent. The only way forward is for all interested in progress to work together: politicians, education, churches, community groups and private firms.

However, hundreds of ventures of many kinds continue to brave the odds. There has been a remarkable growth in worker co-operatives in Britain, five hundred new ventures a year. In 1986, there were one thousand five hundred workers' co-operatives in Britain. An estimated two hundred and fifty thousand may well exist by the year 2000. Most are small, employing less than ten people and almost half those employed are women. A single street in Hackney, East London, is the home of eighteen such co-operatives, employing one hundred people repairing bicycles, cars and TV sets and restoring furniture.

MAKING THINGS

Making money from hobbies is a growing trend. In Canterbury's Main Street, we found three women in their thirties, Nina, Sheila and Polly, operating a spinning and weaving co-operative. Polly said they had had the idea while sitting at the kitchen table. She is a social worker, her husband an architect. To raise £1,200 capital for the shop and the looms, each borrowed £400. No government help was available, even though the city's tourist office considered the venture would be a tourist attraction. In their shop in the Old Weaver's House, the women offer courses in their craft and also sell spinning wheels and knitted articles on commission for clients. Their profits were £150 in a three-day week. They see their work as a social and spiritual activity; customers sometimes return to chat and weave with them. Their oldest weaver is a ninety-two year old woman, one of their keenest, an unemployed postman.

Daily Bread Co-operative in Northampton has been in business since 1980. It was founded by a group of Christian Socialists in Northampton to sell wholefoods, but also to pursue Christian aims of fellowship, fair trading and non-exploitation of workers and of the third world. So far they have been successful in combining spiritual aims with commercial success. They intend to stay a small co-operative, with twenty members and a relatively small turnover of half a million pounds. This small membership means that every worker's views are represented by him or herself.

Britain's inner-city intiatives have their counterpart in other industrialised countries. Puerto Ricans in New York's Lower East Side have taken over derelict buildings and formed homesteading associations. They have planted gardens in vacant lots, established markets and arts centres, installed solar collectors and windmills on rooftops and painted murals. They were helped to move into houses without down-payment, in a scheme called Sweet Equity Urban Homesteading, by the Institute for Social Ecology. According to the Institute's director, Dan Chodorkoff, "these groups were encouraged to create their own forms of leadership and to develop not just the physical rehabilitation of those buildings, but the building of social forms and political forms that can help to empower people as well". (2)

The American Institute for Community Economics has forty community loan funds helping public and private sources to channel money into grassroots community development. Similar initiatives are common in Canada. A community enterprise society of the city of Nanaimo, in British Columbia, set up a community fishing venture which prospered. The society put up part of the capital for each new business in the scheme, leaving the individual owner to find the rest through banks, credit unions and private investors. The society's commitment to the project gives these the incentive to invest. Because of the technical assistance and moral support provided by the agencies, there is a remarkably low failure rate of businesses started in this way. Don Macmillan, co-ordinator of the Nanaimo project, said community economic development had become a 'buzzword'. "Six or seven years ago it was viewed as 'commie talk.' Now it's establishment; you've got the provincial government, you've got the federal government, you've got the Right, you've got the Left". (3)

CITY FARMS

City farms hold great promise for the future. Dozens of these have been founded in recent decades in Britain. These community enterprises make use of derelict sites, provide jobs and teach city children about country life; growing food is not always the primary purpose. Some farms sponsor Youth Training projects through the Manpower Services Commission. Many of these farms are under pressure, as land prices continue to rise and local authorities want open spaces for other purposes. Whether these farms and community gardens will be allowed to survive will be a touchstone of British priorities. The National Federation of City Farms, which has more than sixty member projects, is supported by the Department of the Environment and a wide range of trusts and companies.

Hackney City Farm is among the newest of London city farms. On a tiny site there are pigs, sheep, rabbits, hens, bees, turkeys and guinea pigs, a pottery, a herb garden, a tree nursery and a range of fruits and vegetables. Baby rabbits and guinea pigs support a small animal loan scheme to local schools. "The accent is heavily on traditional, commercial husbandry with strong undertones of social value and education." (4) With finance from Hackney Borough Council, the farm supports a manager, a co-ordinator, a horticulturalist and three others.

On a former scrapyard in Bristol, is Windmill Hill, one of the earliest city farms, which has more than six hundred members. On a visit, Joan Davidson, writing in *The Guardian*, found small allotment gardens let out to people in nearby flats and patients from a local psychiatric hospital. A play centre was operating throughout the week with sessions for preschoolers and the handicapped. A computer and a popular rumpus room were mainly used by disabled children. On weekends and holidays, play schemes were run by volunteers. Women with small children came to print, weave and practise woodwork. The MSC funded job creation programmes at the farm and another twelve jobs were supported by the farm's own fund raising. The Department of Health and Social Security and Avon County Council were paying for two staff members to work with disabled groups in the gardens. Bristol City Council let the site at a peppercorn rent and helped with equipment and vehicles. (5)

The diversity of community projects and co-operatives make it difficult to fit them into specific categories. The Industrial Common Ownership Movement was set up in the seventies and received government support from the Industrial Common Owners Act of 1976. This was followed in 1978 by the National Co-operative Development Agency. However, government support is only as good as the will of the individual in the co-operative . Many co-operatives and community enterprises try to carry through two aims which are difficult to reconcile; making money and providing community benefit and welfare. Co-operatives are relevant for people interested in the quality of life and in control of their own lives, but once the numbers increase co-operatives often run into difficulties.

In the report *Communities in Business*, published by the Centre for Employment Initiatives in August 1986, the conclusion was directed clearly at official policy makers:

> Economic revival. . . is unlikely to bring benefits to the less well-trained, it is unlikely to reach the remote rural areas, and to penetrate the very disadvantaged inner city areas or to revive the old industrial heartlands. It is among these groups, and in such localities that community enterprises are likely to persist. As such they merit understanding and support even though this may require a stretching of the official imagination. . .

LIVING TOGETHER

Rural communities have an unbroken historical tradition stretching from monasteries and secular protest groups to the hippy communes of the 1960 s on both sides of the Atlantic. Hippy communes were various and short-lived, but the demand for community living survives. Today there is a vigorous and solidly-based communes movement, secular and religious. The Communes Network Directory currently lists thirty-seven communities in Britain; they are in three groups: the Communes Network, the Alternative Communities Movement and the Christian Community Movement.(6)

There are many other small groups. Researching on the 'ideological sources of communes in Britain' Jan Bang identified seven strands: co-operative economic relations; appropriate technology; organic agriculture; holistic health; spirituality and personal relationships; the 'paradigm shift'; and radical politics. (7)

Most people living in communes or rural co-operatives are young. Many stay for relatively short periods and quite often they move from one community to another. They choose community life as much for personal reasons as to serve any theory or ideal. This relaxed, á-la-carte attitude suggests that some aspects of communal living might become more widespread, without rigid doctrine or monastic discipline.

We found a down-to-earth and unmonastic atmosphere at Crabapple, near Shrewsbury. The twelve members, with six children, run a profitable wholefood shop in the town centre, selling commune-produced vegetables and eggs and a range of bought-in organic foods. The handsome exterior of Berrington Hall, their 18th century parsonage is carefully maintained, with twenty acres of land farmed as a small-holding. But inside, typical of many communes, the kitchen was scruffy and communal areas looked neglected. The cows, sheep and hens, all in superb condition, were being looked after by Alison, a matter-of-fact and self-confident young woman from Norfolk. She was amused that we took the business of community living so seriously. "All I want is to be involved in managing land in an ecologically sound way, rearing animals in a reasonably humane fashion and sharing resources and skills with a group of people. I've been here five years, but I'm sure not to be ending my days here; very likely I'll join another form of community later."

Paul, also in his twenties, said: "We don't feel part of a movement or that everyone's especially keen to go in our direction. We just want to live a less exploitative life. Some people who meet nothing but alternative-style people get the wrong impression: like the world's already changed. In fact, the world really is still a terrible place". He felt that if the community were to become more prosperous, "it would be nice to have more personal spending money: to go out and have a decent restaurant meal and a pint later. Also we could expand: buy land for afforestation, and not have to worry about raising travel money for political activities like CND". Most members belong to CND, to which the community as a whole is affiliated.

After initially sharing out jobs on roster, Crabapple moved to increased specialisation. Some people run the farm, others run the shop, yet others specialise in building rather than farming. However, everyone works once a week in the shop. One member takes charge of the cooking. Two of the members draw the dole, on the grounds that they are not members of the farm partnership; some have outside jobs, 'to get a bit of air' and these earnings are pooled; everyone gets £5 a week pocket money. Personal savings are frozen during the members' stay, to avoid contrasting living standards, but there are exceptions for special hobbies like photography and for holidays.

This community is clearly successful; one member told us it was becoming 'more of a home and less of a work camp'.

The children all share a room until the age of 10, then have their own rooms. Half the members are vegetarian and this leads to arguments about menus. The community makes cheese and butter and bakes bread. The financial situation is improving. The mortgage on the shop was paid off in 1986, eleven years after the foundation of the community, but loans on the house and the land are still being paid off at £500 a month. The shop and the farm, run as a combined business, make a net profit of around £13,000 a year. Fields are cultivated in rotation; Alison said they were kept, "as clean as possible with no fads about one-straw revolution", a reference to the Japanese-inspired fashion for letting weeds grow. The community is not looking for more members, but visitors are welcome at Crabapple: they pay their keep if they can afford to and also help out.

Lower Shaw Farm, near Swindon in Wiltshire, is a small community that has retained the teaching role that monasteries once had. Its function is to refresh its visitors with the many-sided messages of a wholistic world view. The members do this quite informally, with neither pomposity nor freakishness. The place has a creative untidiness. During a summer week called 'stretching out', assorted activities are taking place in different corners of the farm: circle dancing, massage, shiatsu and yoga. Chickens, a dog, a family of peacocks and various children wander over the terrain. The flowers are untended but grow nonetheless. Only the goats and the donkey are tethered. Course members sleep in converted cowsheds and craft activities take place in the barn. Three couples run the three-acre farm. All members have outside activities centred in groups such as Friends of The Earth, The Well Woman Centre and the Wiltshire Trust for Nature Conservation. They don't see themselves as running the farm full-time because it isn't large enough to support them. Nor do they see themselves as living in any way outside society. Heather, one of the members, explained that most visitors came because they had been before and liked it; a few came through advertisements. Most were active or passive suppporters of peace movements and most were, "sympathetic to vegetarianism even if they don't practise it. In fact a lot of people say that they have become vegetarian through coming here". Heather felt that visitors were, "moving in the same direction. They may chose to come specifically about herbs or woodwork, but they come back because they feel a sympathy with what goes on here, and with the people they meet".

The fact that the local Council has extended their lease for five years was seen by the members as a proof that they were accepted as providing a valuable contribution to the area's resources. This acceptance is all the more remarkable because Lower Shaw farm, until recently on the rural outskirts of Swindon, is now right in the centre of a new housing and industrial estate. An enlightened council sees the farm as a cultural asset. We spoke to Douglas, a regular visitor, who is an Open University lecturer in biology.

> I come here because it's rather nice to do the sort of thing that is usually described as non-scientific. Take something like circle dancing. It's not the sort of thing I would normally do. I have been taught to be suspicious of anything I couldn't prove. Many of the things that go on during some of the courses here—you may not know why they work but they do. That's what is important to me. I begin to change my teaching. I start teaching about herbal medicine rather than just how to identify plants. Then I have been forced to admit we don't understand how some things work. Now perphaps five years ago I wouldn't have liked to admit that in a teaching situation. Now I can say that we don't know and maybe in ten years we'll understand. A lot of that sort of attitude has developed from coming to Shaw. Someone might come to this place for a certain course or a certain person and find something totally different. Nearly everyone who comes to Shaw has something to offer.They may not be a

teacher but quietly in the evening, you'll realize they may be a good counsellor, or good at doing a foot massage or know fungi or just some little thing and suddenly that can become the most important part of the weekend. Some people can't even talk to close friends about what really matters. You come down to Shaw and within half an hour you are talking to a total stranger about quite important things.

Notes:

(1) John Osmond, *Work in the Future*, page 43.

(2) Dan Chodorkoff, Interview, CBC: *New Ideas in Ecology and Economics.*

(3) Don Macmillan, Interview, ibid.

(4) Jonathan Edwards, *City Farmer No 29*. National Federation of City Farms, The Old Vicarage, 66 Fraser Street, Windmill Hill, Bedminster.

(5) Joan Davidson, *The Guardian*, 4/9/85.

(6) *Communes Network*, Laurieston Hall, Castle Douglas, Kirkudbrightshire, Scotland.

(7) ibid.

CHAPTER SIX

Sustainable Development

Near Hassan, Mysore State
Julieta Preston, Government of India Tourist Office

Sustainable Development

WE VISITED a prosperous wheat farm of fifty hectares in the Punjab, where North India's green revolution has become a classic success story of economic development. The bearded farmer sat on his banyan-shaded verandah to welcome us, with many children and grandchildren around him. Later, over an expansive lunch, he told us how useful his children were: each was nominal owner of a part of the farm and thus enabled him to overcome the official land ceiling imposed in the State.

This farmer used to plough with several tractors, but found they were too expensive and always breaking down, so now he up-dated traditional methods and used a pair of white bullocks for each plough, strong animals cross-bred between local and imported strains. The bullocks never broke down and provided enough slurry for biomass electricity to drive the farm's artesian wells and light his house. Because of these advanced methods he considered himself a model farmer and environmentalist and he hoped to encourage other farmers to copy his ideas. His artesian well was properly cemented, with no stagnant pool of water to attract mosquitos and spread malaria.

Our host had little to say about the condition of the three

hundred families who lived in the farm and whose labour drove the bullock teams and hand-weeded the fields. He explained that some of them used to own land, but that in his prosperity he had bought them out. Later that afternoon, we visited the field workers and talked to an old lady and her son. Yes, they had had a small plot, but they had not been able to buy the fertiliser or dig irrigation wells and could not compete with the rich farmer to whom they had eventually sold. Did he pay them well? Neither replied, but both looked eloquently at the newly built guest house on whose verandah we had just taken our lunch.

This visit illustrates the tragic contradictions in the process we call development. Here was myth-making success, where new strain of 'miracle seeds' produced bumper yields, but the peasants on the same land had been further impoverished. Our visit took place some years ago. Since then, more problems have become apparent in the green revolution. Still more peasants have been driven off their land. The dependence on chemical fertilisers and insecticides is producing a plateau effect as the soil and water tables can absorb no more and become polluted and impoverished. These are the contradictions that cause fundamental questions to be asked.

Why, after four decades of economic aid for development, are so many people still hungry? Robert McNamarra, in an address as President of the World Bank, recently spoke of eight hundred million people, more than a sixth of the world's population, "as living in a condition of life so limited by malnutrition, illiteracy, disease, high infant mortality and low life exepectancy as to be beneath any rational definition of human decency".

Critics of industrial society who advocate human-scale and wholistic lifestyles are asking this question too. Their thinking has concerned the third world as much as the first. Fritz Schumacher travelled to India and Burma where he developed his ideas on 'economics as if people mattered' and 'appropriate technology'. Schumacher and his followers' views are now accepted by many people in the third world who experience development at the receiving end. Both parts of our world, developed and undeveloped, can be seen as victims of colonisation; in both, people have had their means of subsistence removed and have become captive consumers in a centralised, industrial economy. Are they better off as a result? We have seen in earlier chapters that more and more people in the industrialised world are counting the cost. In the third world, most people have yet to experience the benefits. More often than not, an aid project will benefit the better-off farmer and further impoverish the women and children of the village. In many countries development has made the poor poorer. We saw how that happened in the Punjab, where the new seed technology, which needs costly irrigation and fertilisers, drove peasants from their lands to be marginalised as landless labourers or join the slum dwellers in the cities. Elsewhere, new dams, ranches and plantations enrich the few and drive the many off the good land, forcing them to over-exploit poorer lands. It is these refugees from development who die when the rains fail.

Radical critics are advocating a grassroots revolution in which people and communities will resume responsibility for their own development. In practice that means using their own resources, relying on traditional knowledge and skills— and reviving them when they are lost—and growing food for themselves rather than export crops.

These critics of current development claim that 'primitive' people, unchanged by development, are not usually hungry and they are rarely ignorant of the things they need to know to survive and even to live well. Ivan Illich observes that the decades of development have mainly served, "to make two billion people define themselves as underdeveloped". Illich defines development in unflattering terms:

... It is the replacement of widespread, unquestioned competence at subsistence activities by the use and consumption of commodities; the monopoly of wage labour over all other kinds of work; redefinition of needs in terms of goods and services mass-produced according to expert design; finally, the rearrangement of the environment in such a fashion that space, time, materials and design favour production and consumption while they degrade or paralyse use-value orientated activities that satisfy needs directly. (1)

The very notion that developing countries could and should somehow catch up with advanced ones is being questioned. Rudolf Bahro rejects the idea of capitalist growth as applied to the developing countries.

It would send the peoples of the third world into a tunnel without an exit, because the living standard they are aiming for is no longer achievable... the imposition of our model on the third world will just lead to the kind of situation I saw in Mexico—first, people move to the shanty-town on the edge of the city, then the next generation can buy a run-down car, trying to reproduce what exists in the metropolis, and so on.(2)

The development process has divided third world peoples into two groups. The Chilean economist, Manfred Maxneef, has observed:

One group consists of people directly or indirectly involved with some kind of development strategy normally designed by the governmental agencies of the country. The other consists of the people, usually the majority, dedicated to designing their own survival strategy. We have also learned that these two segments don't mix; they coexist in a dialectic struggle. Furthermore, the second group has increased, not only in absolute numbers but also relatively.(3)

It is in this second group that the opportunities now lie. In industrial countries, the unemployed in a post-employment society are emerging as pioneers of new lifestyles. The third world is, by definition, full of potential pioneers in this sense. "People in these countries do not have to look for alternative societies", as A.T. Ariyaratne, the Sarvodaya Movement leader in Sri Lanka, said in his 1985 Schumacher Lecture.

Yet the poor of the third world are too often blamed for their own misfortunes, as Michael Redclift and Jonathon Porritt told the 1986 Other Economic Summit:

> Over-grazing, erosion, denuded forests, surface water pollution, mismanagement of natural resources—it is all laid at the feet of the poor. This is a grotesque misrepresentation of the facts. As many have asked, how is it that farmers and herders, who have harmoniously and successfully managed so difficult an environment for hundreds of years, now so suddenly and wilfully destroy it?

Left to themselves, people in the third world can manage far better than the managers suppose. One observer noted in the remote areas of Tanzania:

> There can be good times even when the national economy is depressed, the national debt is growing, international commodity prices are low, and foreign exchange is unavailable... Transport and agricultural support services come to a stop and, when villagers cannot get their food to market—they eat it themselves. (4)

A cruel irony of development occurs when scores of countries in Asia and Africa grow cocoa, coffee, cotton and other crops for export, to pay for development, while their own people go hungry. In these countries, the best agricultural and grazing lands are often cleared to make way for development projects. <u>Development is paid for by aid</u>, which finances projects designed to create surpluses for export, to earn the foreign exchange to service the debts which have been incurred, to pay for development. The vicious circle is completed and starts to revolve again. The governing classes, rich farmers and landlords and the urban elite benefit from this development: the mass of the poor do not. Statistics consistently show there is enough food for all, but the poor cannot afford to buy enough and have been deprived of the land for growing their own. A tragic pattern is seen in famine areas of people starving while there is food in nearby markets.

Ill-conceived development projects can add to, and even cause, ecological disasters. It has been argued that this may well have happened in the recent series of droughts in the African Sahel. Lloyd Timberlake, an acute observer of the African scene, identifies three local ways and one global way in which this could be happening. First, overcultivation, overgrazing and deforestation by stripping the soil of vegetation, increases reflectivity from rocks and bare soil, warms the atmosphere and disperses cloud. Second, the atmosphere could be warmed by additional dust, which reduces the amount of sunshine reaching the earth. Third, lowering of soil moisture could itself suppress rainfall. And globally, the 'greenhouse effect' of excessive carbon dioxide released into the industrial atmosphere by burning large amounts of coal and oil has been found to increase the variability of the climate. Herdsmen who lived before development have coped with droughts for many centuries. As Timberlake concludes, "misuse of the land is widespread, is increasing vulnerability to drought and is reversible".(5) However, this prospect of reversibility gives us some grounds for hope in the continuing desertification of Africa.

IS POPULATION TO BLAME?

Can the problems of development be blamed on the population explosion? It is the readiest scapegoat: many apologists for the development process use it when they say poor countries, 'have to move faster and faster just to stand still'. The argument is that population pressure and not ill-conceived development projects, have driven people to overgraze lands and cut down too many trees for firewood, thereby turning grazing lands into deserts.

Advocates of a grassroots revolution in development turn these arguments upside-down. They argue that when people feel only the negative effects of development, the disruption of their environment and traditional lifestyles, they discover real poverty and come to look upon children as their most valuable economic resource. "The number of children people want is affected by their vulnerability as well as their absolute poverty", Michael Redlift and Jonathon Porritt argued in a TOES lecture. "The conventional argument should be reversed: efforts to slow down population growth will continue to be frustrated unless human needs are met through development."

That development is needed because more people are born is also disputed. It depends what you mean by people, Manfred Maxneef points out. He proposes a new human unit called an *ecoson*, defined by amount of resources he or she needs. "It would not be surprising, for example, to discover that one inhabitant of the United States was equivalent to fifty *ecosons*, and that a single inhabitant of India or Togo was no more than a fraction of an *ecoson*". (6) The implication is that development as we now know it can only increase ecosons and make the population problem worse.

The population problem has not been solved, either by traditional planners or by grassroots economists. Teddy Goldsmith, with other conservative ecologists, argues that people must be motivated to have less children and this has only been achieved when controls have been built into the cultural patterns of traditional societies. (7)

But few critics of current development practices would wish to return to cultural practices like forbidding young widows from remarrying or even burying them alive with their dead husbands, though these practices had an element of birth control as their rationale. Nor would such critics wish to abolish the advances in hygiene and basic medicine that have made spectacular reductions in infant mortality.

There is some polarisation among ecologists and development strategists. In one camp are the birth controllers, subdivided themselves between traditionalists like Goldsmith and enthusiatic family planners using modern methods; in the other camp are liberals who suspect that family planning for the third world may ultimately be intended to perpetuate the conditions for extravagant consumerism among the rich. From a middle position, Jonathon Porritt, speaking as chairman of Friends of the Earth, calls for a quite honest acceptance that long-term reductions of population of both North and South are a critical precondition for green politics being successful:

There is an instant knee-jerk response from so many people in the development movement, that those who talk about population only do it to draw a veil over the much more complicated issues of distribution of wealth, food, social justice and so on. That's hopelessly anachronistic. In the old days, the advocates of long-term population reduction did their cause no good whatsoever, using intemperate and patronising language that did imply a sense of wishing to keep down the breeding. This approach now has no currency in the Green movement. For us, readiness to see wealth distribution and sustainable development as part of a long-term population reduction is absolutely essential. You can't say the problem resides exclusively in the third world: it also resides in the first world, where our celebrated consumption patterns mean that for every 12 people living in Nepal you only need one person living in the West. And if you're quite logical about this, the implication is that therefore we ought to be 12 times as concerned about population levels. (Interview with the authors, 1986) (8)

In the first stage of industrial development, stable populations begin to expand. This happened in Europe from the 18th century. In a secondary phase, economic security, education and access to birth control bring the rates down again. China is a model for the developing world, a country where stringent birth control legislation has surely been only a secondary factor in bringing population growth under control: the crucial factor, and the most striking contrast with India, has been the ability of the Chinese system to abolish destitution. At the other end of the spectrum the African population explosion, currently the worst in the world, would appear to be the result at least as much as the cause, of the failure of development to trickle down to the poor, who feel only its disruptive effects as their forests, lakes, rivers and grazing lands are confiscated or poisoned. The world's family planners have also recognised that effective programmmes have to work at village level; they cannot be imposed from above. Each community has collectively to appreciate the need in its own area for smaller families. Once again, we are brought back to the need to restore community life and action.

LADAKH

Development can destroy a sustainable way of life, even if it comes at second hand—that is, if it originates from a country which is itself in the third world. This is happening at the peripheries of most third world countries as modernisation crosses the last frontiers. It is happening in

Ladakh, where the destruction of a culture has been closely observed by Helena Norberg-Hodge. Helena belongs to the wholistic movement and is at work in Ladakh trying to halt the destruction. The anti-development project of which she is a prime mover, has been recognised by the Right Livelihood Foundation Award for 1986.

Ladakh is a mountain-locked kingdom between the Himalayas and the Karakorams. A poor soil and very low rainfall have nurtured a frugal and sturdy culture. Helena Norberg-Hodge experiences Ladakh as a classically wholistic culture. It has a sense of dependent origination in which nothing exists independently of anything else. She observes that this is true also of peoples' notion of themselves, which lacks the Western preoccupation with an 'ego' existing independently of other people and of nature. The majority of Ladakhis are Buddhists, who have lived in harmony with the Muslim minority and the handful of missionized Christians. There is an intellectual tradition in the monasteries, but the Buddhism of the people is a folk religion perfectly integrated with the environment. The most destructive impact has been from Indian trade and Western tourism. On an early visit in 1974, Helena was shown round Tingosgang village by a young man whom she asked out of curiosity to show her the poorest house. We don't have any poor houses here he replied. Eight years later she overheard the same man telling a Western tourist: "if you could only help us Ladakhis. We're so poor . . ."For Helena, the incident illustrates how pride and self-respect were giving way to a sense of insecurity and inferiority.

Ladakhis used to make their bricks from mud, an abundant and cheap local material which people used for building durable and beautiful houses. But the intrusion of modernity, encouraged by Indian trade and advertising, has discredited mud in favour of cement, which has to be dragged across the Himalayas and is used to construct ugly, single-storey buildings in and around Leh, the capital. As more houses were built in Leh, local mud became scarce and imported cement was used instead. Helena showed us the photograph of a fine three-storey farm house built of mud bricks, surrounded by its screen of trees. She contrasted this with the box-like cement house to which the family had moved. However, not all the family had moved: in the modern house there was no room for the old grandmother so she was left behind.

Money played a minimal part in Ladakh before it was opened to outside influence. Nor did the harshness of the environment impose unremitting toil. Even in the four month summer harvest season, when food for the rest of the year had to be brought in and stored, there was time for laughter and conviviality and during the eight winter months there was ample leisure for ritual, storytelling, parties and meetings. Today the pressure of demand for new products and a money-centred lifestyle threatens to abolish leisure.

Helena describes the role of schools in transforming the Ladakhis' view of the world. She sees this as training people who already know how to support themselves to become urban consumers. When a Ladakhi is taught to build as an engineer, his skills in building mud houses are lost. In the schools the children are not taught how to grow barley at fourteen thousand feet, or to breed yaks. Helena believes that unless alternatives to hi-tech development are presented and adopted within ten years, a totally corrupted and dependent population will have been created. Her Ladakh Project, which supports the Ladakh Ecological Development Group, has been able to gain the support and help of influential Ladakhis. One Ladakhi farmer who had been using pesticides was persuaded to return to the traditional organic farming of the region. The Group's working committee consists of Ladakhis who want to see small-scale, appropriate technologies restored or adopted. They have already installed over one hundred and thirty 'trombes'—black-painted, south-facing walls behind glass windows, which can absorb enough solar heat to keep a room close to fourteen degrees celsius in sub-zero weather. There have been successful experiments using solar ovens, a ram water pump and other artifacts designed to help people maintain a sustainable, decentralized society, meeting its own basic needs. The ultimate aim is for the region to take the best that modern technology offers, while retaining a traditional way of life and values that people in the West are only now groping towards regaining.

THE GRASSROOTS APPROACH

What is the most promising way out of the development dilemma, in which official aid, trade and inappropriate technology help the few and leave the many at best untouched, or even further impoverished? The juggernaut seems unstoppable because so many vested interests are involved: third world governments who often need the aid to stay in power; export lobbies; banking lobbies; the powerful industries that benefit: grains, fertilisers, pesticides, heavy machinery, and armaments; the urban middle classes in the third world who buy the luxury imports so often bought with money earned by cash crop exports.

Critics in the wholistic movement want both first and third worlds to change their priorities and values. Writers on the new economics look forward to a time when industrial societies will become less voracious of energy and raw materials and more globally-minded. When people live more natural lives and do more of their 'ownwork', James Robertson argues, there will be "the prospect of a new path of self-reliant economic development—'another development'—no less for the poor countries than for the rich". (9)

Meanwhile, the development process is in a schizophrenic period, driven forward by vested interests while more and more misgivings are expressed, both at the giving and at the receiving ends of the process. Even the

World Bank, which has done more than any other body to finance ecologically and socially destructive projects, has modified some of its projects in response to criticism.

Undeterred by doubt, the official 1985 Economic Summit of rich countries in Bonn placed 'sustained economic growth' in the developed world at the head of its priorities, as well as the 'signficant expansion of world trade, enabling LDCs (less developed countries) to increase their export earnings'. It called for 'flexible rescheduling of international debts whilst the LDCs begin to achieve trade surpluses', omitting to mention that it is the rich countries' industries and banking systems that have mainly profited from development aid and that these would collapse if the debts were repudiated, which is what would have to happen if they were not rescheduled.

However, for the first time the Summit communique had a section on environmental policies, including an attack on desertification in Africa. An international plan of action to combat desertification had already been launched in 1977 at a projected cost of thirty billion dollars over twenty years. But only a tiny proportion of that has been disbursed and meanwhile, as Michael Redclift and Jonathon Porritt concluded at the 1986 meeting of The Other Economic Summit (TOES), quite simply the fight against desertification is being lost. They said nearly seven million square kilometres of subsaharan Africa, an area twice as big as India, was under direct threat of desertification through over-grazing. (10)

More and more third world leaders and officials are paying at least lip-service to the emerging concept of real needs as opposed to development-induced wants. But can people in power be expected to break the system on which their power rests? In the third world no less than the first, economic development is an alliance of political and economic interests. Teddy Goldsmith, a radical critic of the concept of economic development, had this in mind during a stormy international meeting on the issue, when half-ironically he offered the only solution he could see: "Wipe out the debt—interest as well as capital; stop aid—which is only a subsidy for super-colonialist third world governments; and ban the export of cash crops". *(The Guardian 16/6/85)*

For the longer term the emerging grassroots solution was defined at the same meeting of the Society for International Development by its general secretary, Mr Ponna Wignaraja, as participatory development, where people who have hitherto been marginalised become subjects and actors in the process. A movement of grassroots-minded writers, planners and activists is emerging throughout the third world.

Some components of this movement are not new. The Gandhian-inspired Chipko movement in India, in which peasant women hugged trees to save them from the axe, dates from colonial times and has now spread throughout India. This and many parallel movements had its origins among people for whom the forest provides fruits, nuts, animal fodder, green manure and fuel. For such people the forest provides a cultural as well as a physical background. Chipko protests began when the British introduced modern forest management and commercial exploitation. Today, their protest is against large-scale expropriation of agricultural or grazing land for dams and the encroachment on traditional fishing rights by industrial trawling. Chipko people spread their ideas through poems, Gandhian fasts and long marches. What began as Gandhian satyagrahas in defence of forests, has now developed into a protest against insensitive economic development. An Indian academic report describes the villagers' plight:

> Villages that were self sufficient in food had to resort to food imports as a result of declining food productivity. This, in turn, was related to the reduction of soil fertility in the forests. Water resources began to dry up as the forests disappeared. The so-called 'natural disasters,' such as floods

and landslides, began to occur in river systems which had hitherto been stable. (11)

Such movements are not confined to India. The National Council of the Women of Kenya set up the Green Belt Movement which has planted hundreds of thousands of seedlings in over seven hundred greenbelts. In doing so, they had to rediscover inter-cropping and agroforestry techniques that had been supplanted by modern plantation and farming methods. Communities and schoolchildren help with the planting and 'Greenbelt Rangers' guard the seedlings.

Gandhi defined his idea of swadeshi as follows:

I must not serve my distant neighbour at the expense of the nearest...Swadeshi is that spirit in us which restricts us to the use and service of our immediate surroundings to the exclusion of the more remote...It would be your duty and mine to find our neighbours who can supply our wants, and teach them to supply them where they do not know how to proceed, assuming that they are neighbours who are in want of healthy occupation. Then every village of India will almost be a self-supporting and self-contained unit, exchanging only such necessary commodities with other villages which are not locally producable.

In Sri Lanka the Sarvodaya Shramadana Movement, inspired by this ideal, operates in over seven thousand small communities. The movement's name means 'the awakening of all through mutual sharing.' A.T. Atariyaratne outlined its aims in his 1985 Schumacher Lecture:

Not to build an alternative society, but to proceed from the old society, that is from where we are, to a post-modern society in a continuum. We have named this a 'no-poverty society', and we propose to by-pass the modern society, which we believe is neither sustainable nor possible for all people in the world to attain.

The movement began with an extensive study programme in disadavantaged villages, and later began a community development programme which now involves the lives of two and a half million people in one out of every three Sri Lankan villages. Children as well as adults are involved in training for economic and cultural self-reliance.

These movements are resisted by the vested interests they challenge. They are often represented as standing for ecology, which is presented as a luxury as against the claims of development. This is a political struggle, as Smitu Kothari, the Indian ecological activist, explained in a paper called *Ecology Versus Development—the Struggle for Survival*. He said the backlash against grassroots development took the form of 'vilification, inspired mass hysteria against individuals and groups, attempts to divide resistance by offering concessions and, when all else fails, outright lawless repression'. Faced with that and the indifference of many local and state governments to social problems, Kothari concluded:

> This movement needs links at all levels, from the local to the
> international . . . because fundamentally, these efforts question
> a system which perpetuates over-consumption by a few
> instead of satisfying the basic needs of many, and in which
> there is a transfer of production from, for instance, artisans to
> resource and energy-intensive industries incapable of
> absorbing those that they displace.

Rajni Kothari, in his acceptance speech of the Right Livelihood Foundation award in 1985, described his Lokayan grassroots discussion and activisation groups as a movement away from specialized knowledge to what we call social knowledge:

> Lokayan has moved away from the cool and amoral

conception of scientific objectvity which does not allow one to take sides... Lokayan conceives of the knowledge process as one of participation and involvement of diverse people, not just academics and intellectuals, but activists, professionals and politicians as well. There is also a feminist input into our whole thinking on politics. It has not just enlarged the scope of politics by bringing into its ambit what was until recently considered a personal and a private world. From a position that the personal and the political are polar opposites to one that 'personal is political', on to the position that political is personal' is a massive shift, not just in the position of women in politics but in our whole understanding of politics as such.

Notes:

(1) Illich, *Shadow Work*, page 20.
(2) Bahro, *From Red to Green*, page 211.
(3) Inglis, *The New Economic Agenda*, page 144.
(4) Adi Asono, *Development*, 1983 no 3.
(5) Timberlake, *Africa in Crisis*, page 31.
(6) Maxneef, *From the Outside Looking In*, page 53.
(7) Goldsmith, *The Stable Society*, page 85.
(8) Interview with the authors, 1986.
(9) Robertson, *Future Work*.
(10) *Why Bankrupt the Earth?*, TOES 1986.
(11) ibid.

CHAPTER SEVEN

Appropriate Technology

Solar Wall: Centre for Alternative Technology, Machynlleth, Denis Thorpe, The Guardian

Appropriate Technology

SCHUMACHER'S most influential idea, in both the third world and the industrialised world, has been that of appropriate technology. The alienation of factory workers, satirised in Charlie Chaplin's film *Modern Times*, has already passed into folklore. Schumacher was the first to develop a theory of the dynamics of technology, showing how a willing servant has become a tyrannical master and how industrial man is imposing the same master on others.

Strange to say, technology, although of course the product of man, tends to develop by its own laws and principles, and these are very different from those of human nature or of living nature in general. Nature always, so to speak, knows where and when to stop. Greater even than the mystery of natural growth is the mystery of natural cessation of growth. There is measure in all natural things—in their size, speed or violence. As a result, the system of nature, of which man is a part, tends to be self-balancing, self-adjusting, self-cleansing. Not so with technology, or perhaps I should say: not so with man dominated by technology and specialisation. Technology recognises no self-limiting principle—in terms, for instance, of size, speed or violence. It therefore does not possess the virtue of being self-balancing, self-adjusting and self-cleansing. In the subtle system of nature, technology, and in particular the super-technology of the modern world, acts like a foreign body, and there are now numerous signs of rejection.(1)

The problem is the same under capitalist and socialist regimes. In *Good Work,* Schumacher shows that unless the technological base is modified, neither system can change for the better. "Mindless work in office or factory is equally mindless under any system." He takes issue with an Iranian who said his country should seek the West's technology, not its ideology. "Is this not a bit like saying: I want to import eggs for hatching but I don't want chicks from them but mice or kangaroos."(2)

Schumacher developed these ideas on visits to India in the sixties, a time when that country was firmly set on its path of big-industry development. He came back with the story of a third world country blessed with many small brickworks. Along come aid and development to install a large, modern, mass-producing brickworks. The small rural brickworks are killed by the competition and the workers are made redundant.

Taking rich and poor countries into the same field of vision, Schumacher proposed technology fulfil three conditions: cheap enough so that it is accessible to virtually everyone; suitable for small-scale application; and compatible with people's need for creativity. (3)

With his friend George MacRobie, Schumacher founded the Intermediate Technology Group in 1965 as an attack on what he called the 'law of the disappearing middle'—the space in between the impracticably large and the impotently small. Today, the Group is part of a world-wide network of appropriate technology. West Germany, France, the Netherlands and the Scandinavian countries all have their own groups and the Americans have sponsored the

Appropriate Technology International.

McRobie, who is still in the same job, recently reported steady progress in the spread of appropriate technology. In India people in many areas were being trained, "to make and mend pumps, bicycles, simple rural equipment of different kinds. If the local resources are leather, they start developing footwear. There are small-scale spinning machines...Over two million people are getting pure water from small pumps developed over ten years; there are more than forty firms in India producing them..." (4)

In his own book *Small is Possible*, McRobie shows how these ideas have now spread from the poor countries to the rich ones, beginning in the poorer areas of the latter:

> It is characteristic of such territories that they closely resemble colonies (which produce, as someone put it, what they do not consume, and consume what they do not produce); and the faster the metropolitan centre that controls them grows, the more rapidly they deteriorate. If they are to do more than merely survive with the aid of welfare payments, such communities need technologies appropriate to their resources and their lifestyles. (5)

This idea has begun to take root in post-industrial society, where people have lost their old skills as well as their old jobs and are being encouraged to develop intermediate, human-scale technology. Mike Cooley, Technical Director of the Greater London Enterprise Board, is a pioneer in this field. He was leader of the Lucas Airospace shop stewards who tried, in the seventies, to switch production from arms to useful products. At GLEB, Cooley has offered workspace to 'barefoot' scientists, getting away from what he calls throwaway mass-production—things designed to break down and wear out. His answer was to foster mildly subversive forms of production: cars built to last and washing machines without the plastic parts that are deliberately designed to wear out. GLEB has set up technology networks in London polytechnic colleges. These bring together community workshops and academic researchers, provide workshop space for developing prototypes and inject 'pump-priming' finance.

Mike Cooley's projects at GLEB have included work on a lathe that can be operated in a personal and creative way, a portable kidney dialysis machine, a power-assisted bicycle, a body structure for cars that gives them longer life. Cooley told us that workers can play a greater role in the design process:

> To counteract technologies designed to de-skill and displace workers, we need democratic decision-making to enhance skills. At workplaces we must get away from the notion of one best way to do a thing. We have had disabled people designing a database of treatment options: that gave them some independence from the expert. They designed and built their own exercise machines—far better for the job than anything on offer. (6)

APPROPRIATE ENERGY

At the heart of the technology debate is the problem of energy. The United States and the Soviet Union, with 10.6 per cent of the world's population, consume 43.4 per cent of global energy; the average third world citizen uses up 0.5 per cent of a ton of oil equivalent a year, while the average Canadian consumes 8.8 tons. Until very recently, industrial growth and energy-use progressed together inexorably. The oil crises of the seventies reversed this trend through the combined effects of conservation and industrial recession. A sharp fall in oil prices followed, that opened the way to a return of the old profligacy. This is short-sighted behaviour, as oil remains a dwindling resource. More than half of proved reserves are in the Middle East, a region which could once again hold the rest of the world to ransom in the 1990s, when non-OPEC petroleum is expected to decline.

Now is the time to ask: energy for what? The Chernobyl accident of 1986 demonstrated the frightening dangers of nuclear power. If our society cannot function without energy that can only be produced in this way, is it not time to change that society? Nuclear energy is the ultimate expression of mankind's continual flight forwards; its use contains risk factors on which the odds are increasing. Yet, instead of turning towards greater conservation and use of renewable energy, governments in Britain, France and elsewhere (though no longer in the United States) continue placing their hopes in nuclear energy. This energy is already in its second phase, since uranium its raw material, is a finite resource. The industry is poised to move on from thermal reactors to fast breeders. In theory these can multiply energy reserves sixty times through breeding plutonium from non-fissile U-238. But no convincing solution has been found to the problems of reprocessing the highly radioactive wastes involved. The magazine *The Ecologist* pointed out that, "any loss of plutonium in the fast breeder fuel cycle drastically threatens the efficiency of breeding and will inevitably contaminate the environment with one of the most dangerous radiotoxins known to man". The magazine calculates that fastbreeder reactors have the potential for causing not only chemical explosions, which would release far greater quantities of radiation than Chernobyl did, but atomic explosions too, "a terrifying thesis that the nuclear industry has yet to rebuff". (7)

Nuclear power has been represented as a relatively cheap form of energy, but ample evidence suggests that costs have been grossly and deliberately understated by electricity authorities for the sake of the propaganda they need to secure financing. Government, too, has had a hidden vested interest in nuclear energy because of the industry's close association with nuclear weapons. On one occasion, the British Central Electricity Generating Board's cost statistics forgot to account for inflation. Real costs have been distorted: hidden research subsidies from military budgets, unacknowledged purchases of weapons-grade plutonium for bomb-making, underestimated costing for decommissioning (probably as costly as construction, but nobody knows, for it has scarcely been tried) and waste disposal and security. In Britain and France, nuclear power has enjoyed almost unlimited funding: £2.2 billion on Britain's fast breeder prototype and almost £3 billion on the French Superphoenix, yet nuclear power still produces only four per cent of British energy. In France, an unparalleled crash programme of nuclear construction was designed to cut down oil bills, but in the nine years from 1973, the French succeeded in cutting oil imports by significantly less than the British and Dutch, who had much smaller nuclear power programmes. The best indication that nuclear power does not pay comes from the United States, where Wall Street, not the taxpayer, has had to find the money. The result is that nuclear power construction in the United States has virtually come to a halt.

Nuclear power is much more dangerous than is officially admitted. The worst danger is that it encourages nuclear weapons proliferation. The intimate links with military purposes at various stages of the process make it virtually certain that some third world importers of nuclear technology and materials will go on to make bombs. Added to that is the danger of terrorist threats, or actual use of nuclear weapons and of attacks with conventional weapons on nuclear power stations. The likely fate of nuclear power stations in war, even conventional war, is discussed too rarely. If a prospect should arise of serious nuclear disarmament by the Superpowers, nuclear power stations would remain sitting ducks for conventional attacks. A single successful hit would make the Chernobyl explosion look like a fireworks party.

Misgivings on nuclear energy were openly expressed at the time of the Chernobyl accident, but they have subsided. What happened and what might easily have happened was deliberately understated, because of governments' nuclear commitments in the West as well as the Soviet Union. Dr Richard Webb, the American nuclear hazards expert, calculated that potential cancer deaths from gamma radiation alone from the Chernobyl accident could number between two hundred and eighty thousand and seven hundred and twenty thousand in the next thirty or forty years, in an area of six hundred thousand square kilomtres stretching across Scandinavia and north-central Europe. (8)

Only fifteen per cent of the damaged Chernobyl reactor's core was vaporised and favourable winds helped blow the cloud away from many parts of Europe. Even so, after the accident radiation levels in Europe were five times higher than those reached during above-ground nuclear testing in the 1950s and 1960s. Such a disaster could not happen in the West we were told, yet it has since been demonstrated that the latest light water reactors used in the West are actually more dangerous, because an explosion in these could burst open any containment. The United States Nuclear Regulatory Commssion estimated one chance in two of a serious nuclear acci dent in the USA before the end of the century. *The Ecologist* infers from this that since the USA has twenty-five per cent of the reactors, the world may expect a serious nuclear accident once every eight years. (9)

Nuclear power represents the opposite of human-centred development. It marks a decisive move towards a more centralised, secretive and authoritarian society, because of the need for intense security surrounding all parts of the nuclear process. A human-centred society would use less energy. People and goods would no longer have to travel great distances every day; required energy would be produced at local or bio-regional level in the form best suited to local resources and needs.

A society seeking to move towards human-scale organisations would immediately scrap nuclear energy. The alternatives are conservation, renewable energy and more judicious use of oil, coal (using anti-pollution filters) and other fossil fuels. Energy conservation has hardly started. It could bring more substantial economic gains in Britain, France, West Germany and other nuclear-energy States. Its development could create many more jobs. The high proportion of heat currently wasted in power generation could be harnessed for use in Combined Heat and Power systems. The method has proven potential; the only obstacle is lack of official funding. The same appplies to solar energy in warmer climates and wave energy and fresh water energy in Britain and other colder countries.

A great variety of experimental and operational projects in wind, wave, solar, biomass and other sources of renewable energy exist all over the world. These sources account for only eighteen per cent of world energy use, one per cent more than in 1973, when the oil crisis began. Since that same year, the share of nuclear energy has risen from one per cent to three per cent of world output, while the share of oil has gone down from fifty-six to thirty-five per cent.

An analysis called *Energy-Efficient Futures*, conducted with the support of the British Department of Energy and the European Commission, showed in 1986 that within thirty years Britain could supply two-thirds of its needs from renewable resources, exploiting its energy four times more efficiently, (*The Times 26/5/86*). Yet a dogged commitment to nuclear power, which enjoys development grants of £250 million a year, caused the cessation of a modest £14 million devoted to renewable sources. British pioneering work on wave and tidal energy was suspended through lack of funding, leaving the field open to Norwegians, who are making and exporting this equipment. Another promising British technique, Ocean Thermal Energy Conversion, converts the thermal energy of warm ocean surfaces into electricity. As this happens large amounts of nutrient-rich waters are brought to the surface, so that a plant's locality can be used for large scale aqua-culture, ranging from conventional fish-farming to highly specialised microbially-based protein.

An even more promising technology pioneered in Britain is the production of large-scale fuel cells, whose fuel can be bio-generated gases, but research grants and funding have stopped, so the technique is being developed in Japan. The *Guardian's* science correspondent, Anthony Tucker, blamed, "national energy monopolies and the government departments which serve them, who are pegged to narrow commitments and to national policies which savagely discount technologies whose perceived parochial role is small". (10) In Britain and other countries bent on nuclear power, the initiative for renewable energy is usually taken by individuals, firms or small communities, whose aim is usually to promote local self-reliance and save money. In South Wales the Newport and Nevern Energy Group began informally in 1980, when residents in the two rural parishes calculated that every year some £250,000 was leaving their community in energy costs. They began with bulk purchases of loft insulating equipment and moved on to harnessing local streams and solar energy. The two sources are complementary, since stronger water pressure in winter compensates for the lack of sunshine. (11) An urban equivalent to the Newport and Nevern Group is the Future City Home established at the same time at 101, Philip Street, Bristol, also called the Urban Centre for Appropriate Technology. It specialises in advanced forms of insulation and solar panels.

Characteristic of informal, British muddling through is the well-known Centre for Alternative Technology at Machynlleth in North Wales. On a visit in 1985 on its tenth anniversary ,we watched windmills that work alongside those that didn't. Weeds flourished amongst the organic plots to show they did more good than harm. This is the only community in the world that lives off solar, water and wind energy and manages to explain how it works in words of mostly one syllable. A sign on a plastic bin in the organic waste-collection area says: 'Please Pee Here'. A bigger tank is labelled: 'Nothing happens here. For years we tried a solar-heated carp pond. It did not work'. Another carp pond does work, on the direct light of the fitful Welsh sun and nearby is Britain's only inter-seasonal solar heat store. It works. A windmill made from an old bicycle wheel can recharge batteries or work an agricultural fence. A huge, new windmill on the mountain keeps the whole community supplied with power when pressure at the water-wheel is low.

In the early days there had been hopes of setting up alternative universities, chains of organic farms, centres all over the world. The founders had dreamed of communities supplied by windmills, solar panels and organic vegetable growing. The result has been a more modest teaching community, living on its gate money from visitors and research contracts for some of its projects. In its teaching role it received half a million visitors in the first ten years which fulfilled a basic aim of its founder, Gerard Morgan-Grenville. "Unless the Western world could pioneer for itself some way in which life could be lived without using up the capital resources of planet earth, the collapse of civilisation was ultimately inevitable," he said. Ten years on, the pioneers are established: twenty eight full-time staff, with thirteen of them with six children living as a community inside the old quarry. There has, however, been no obvious breakthrough to the outside world. The Central Electricity Generating Board still considers itself the only serious power source.

"Enough water runs off our hilly regions to provide all the power they need—but nobody bothers, because the grid exists", said Bob Todd, the centre's technical director. Todd endlessly adapts his systems to Welsh rain and cold and supplies prototypes to remote Scottish islands and energy-starved communities around the world. His unique interseasonal heat store warms the exhibition hall, free, up to

Christmas. "We could have it working all the year round if we could modify it some more, but there isn't the money." Todd left his job as lecturer in engineering control systems in revolt against the technological push in industry, inventing things people didn't want and creating markets for them. The technical push carries on, while the Department of Energy's renewable energy research budget has actually been cut since the centre was founded.

ARE COMPUTERS APPROPRIATE?

The advocates of a human-centred, decentralised world are not always united about technology. What will be the role of specialised, hi-technology medicine in a health service based on community clinics? What kind of national transport system is desirable in a decentralised economy based on 'ownwork' and renewable energy?

Will the revolt from the mass-produced, throwaway society be putting back the clock too far for commonsense? We can now buy a reliable Japanese electronic watch for as little as £1 .99, designed to be thrown away when the battery runs out after about a year. Repair or maintenance of old-fashioned watches might be difficult to justify, nor would many people prefer to bring back clockwork.

Most people in the 'small-is-beautiful' movement are not anarchists, so there will be a role for central and regional authority and some specialisation in technology and industry. But people in the movement do insist on strict criteria: technology will need to pass Schumacher's tests; specialisation must be proved as serving the true interests of the community. Battery watches, transistor radios, hospitals for special diseases and major surgery and national transport systems will surely survive in the new society.

Computers are especially controversial. They help both sides, the centralisers and the decentralisers. Policemen, civil servants and industrialists all want our names on their data banks. On the other hand, computers can enable us to work at home instead of commuting to an office. They can give us information previously monopolised by experts and they can put us in touch with others through networks. Networks could develop political significance as people attempt to use them for decentralisation. Information is exchanged between individuals and groups and once you are in a network, secrecy and bureaucracy are eliminated.

David Hopson is building up a computer network called UNET. He was one of the organisers of the British Unemployed Resource Network (BURN), which supported self-help groups and initiatives and amassed a vast store of paper-based information. BURN was discontinued after five years, but at the final meeting, everyone agreed that computers could do the job better. The authors of this book are on-line in UNET and we received a message from David on his theory and practice for this chapter:

> Employment is merely one technology for doing work, and must now take its place alongside other, perhaps novel technologies for the creation of wealth, which include such things as prosumption, (production—consumption), ownwork etc. BURN's experience during its five years of operation was that all successful unemployment groups have eventually become community projects or local enterprise initiatives. Accordingly, UNET is concerned with supporting Community, Church and Voluntary organisations as well as those more directly identifiable with unemployed people. UNET offers electronic mail, information management and consultancy. It has brought on-line well-defined networks, like Church Community Programme agents, local—regional information providers like the Swindon Unemployment Movement, and Cornwall and Devon Unemployment Resource Network. UNET shares bulletin-board facilities with GREENET, another network comprising green-thinking

groups and individuals. Twenty UNET users were due to be on-line by the end of 1986, with a projected take-up of 200 by the end of 1987—an estimate based on the relationship single users and the networks they represent. Its practical value was demonstrated when members found housing improvement schemes ran up against trades union objections in some areas —an effective veto under Community Project rules—but not in other areas. The network achieved a coherent national view of what was happening, and developed a strategy for gaining the necessary union support everywhere. Hitherto such issues could only be addressed workshops, annual conferences, or in publications where communication is one-way.

UNET operates with four full-time workers on a grant of £10,000 a year as well as an income for services provided. It has links with Canada, Germany and Holland and potential links with twenty other countries. Systems of this kind are ideally suited for international networking, showing that appropriate technology does not need to imply a narrow regionalism. As a technology, computors are ideally suited to fit in with a 'think globally, act locally' mentality.

Notes:

(1)   Schumacher, *Small is Beautiful,* page 122.
(2)   Schumacher, *Good Work,* page 41.
(3)   McRobie, *Small is Possible.*
(4)   Interview CBC *New Ideas in Ecology and Economics.*
(5)   McRobie, op cit, page 75.
(6)   Interview with authors. 1986.
(7)   *The Ecologist Vol.16. No.4-5* 1986.
(8)   ibid.
(9)   Ibid.
(10) Anthony Tucker, *The Guardian 9/9/86.*
(11) ibid.

CHAPTER EIGHT

Deep Ecology

Beech Trees Damaged by Acid Rain, New Forest
Martin Argles, The Guardian

Deep Ecology

Ecology is like a crystal prism; its facets illuminate wholistic thinking. As a science, it describes the interaction of animate and inanimate forces; as a philosophy it seeks to interpret the place of man and other animals within nature. The facet of environmentalism signifies care and commitment to protect the earth and with the concept of wilderness, modern ecology offers us a deeply needed link with our remote origins. And the vision of *Gaia*, half scientific, half poetic, shows the whole earth as a living organism.

In the facets of this crystal, we see reflected what we choose. Is nature a relentless battle between competing species, a divinely structured arcadia of co-operation, or only the granary of resources for human advancement? Ecology offers no solutions, practical or idealistic, to the problems of our age; its deepest aim is not knowledge but awareness.

The ambiguity is necessary, enabling ecology to escape from the compartmentalisation and reductionism of other sciences. In searching for values, ecology challenges traditional notions of both science and religion. Its call has been heard for centuries, but our age, the first to threaten the survival of the whole environment, has become the age of ecology.

A fundamental distinction runs through the whole of contemporary ecological thinking: the difference between the shallow ecologists (or environmentalists) and the deep ecologists. The environmentalist accepts the intellectual framework of industrial society and seeks to solve environmental problems as they arise within that context; the deep ecologist considers that no such problems can be solved without changing our system of values. In the eyes of the deep ecologist, our civilisation has taken a wrong turning. Fritjof Capra defines the distinction:

> Whereas shallow environmentalism is concerned with more efficient control and management of the natural environment for the benefit of 'man', the deep ecology movement recognizes that ecological balance will require profound changes in our perception of the role of human beings in the planetary ecosystem. In short, it will require a new philosophical and religious basis. (1)

Here is a table of the two contrasting attitudes, drawn up by the first of the deep ecologists, the Norwegian, Arne Naess: (2)

SHALLOW ECOLOGY	DEEP ECOLOGY
Natural diversity is valuable as a resource for us.	Natural diversity has its own intrinsic value.
It is nonsense to talk about value except as value for mankind.	Equating 'value' with value for humans' reveals a social prejudice.
Plant species should be saved because of their value as genetic reserves for human agriculture and medicine.	Plant species should be saved because of their intrinsic value.

Pollution should be decreased if it threatens economic growth.	Decrease of pollution has priority over economic growth.
Third world population growth threatens ecological equilibrium.	World population at level threatens eco-systems, but the population and behaviour of industrial states does so more than that of any others. Human population today is excessive.
'Resource' means resource for humans.	'Resource' means resource for living beings.
People will not tolerate a broad decrease in their standard of living.	People should not tolerate broad decrease in the quality of life but in the standard of living in over-developed countries.
Nature is cruel and necessarily so.	Man is cruel but not necessarily so.

The deep ecologist draws a necessarily radical conclusion from the discipline. The American ecologist Michael McCloskey, director of the Sierra Club, stated his own conclusion in 1970:

A revolution is truly needed—in our values, outlooks and economic organisation. For the crisis in our environment stems from a legacy of economic and technical premises which have been pursued in the absence of ecological knowledge. That other revolution, the industrial one that is turning sour, needs to be replaced by a revolution of new attitudes towards growth, goods, space and living things. (3)

Donald Worster, the historian of Anglo-American ecology, saw the challenge of McCloskey and others as directed at nothing less than:

> The world view of the aspiring middle class, with its dedication to technology, unlimited production and consumption, self-advancement, individualism, and the domination of nature. Time had run out on these modern-age values: nature's economy had been pushed to the breaking point, and 'ecology' was to be the rallying cry of the revolution. (4)

The unique feature of this protest against the scientific-industrial-technological mindset, as Worster observes, is that, "it has been led not by poets or artists as in the past, but by individuals from within the scientific community...In turning to a branch of science as a panacea for the ills brought about by science, we encounter the ultimate paradox of the Age of Ecology". (5)

The essential challenge of deep ecology is on the question of values, as the zoologist, Neil Evernden, explains:

> When you speak of environment, that automatically presupposes that all the value, all the life part, has been scraped off...Once there's no involvement, once there's no interaction with it, it's just that stuff. And to describe someone as an environmentalist, then, is to describe someone who is interested in 'that stuff'. And that in turn, I think is misleading, because what the original experience of that individual was that led him or her to this concern was not 'that stuff', but one's relationship to it, one's involvement with it as a field of self, if you like. One's feeling of being a part...So ironically, the very concept of environment reveals an attitude which prevents one ever being part, of ever accomplishing what the original motivation is to the environmentalist, namely a personal, deep commitment to place.

This attitude marks the profound differences between deep ecologists and environmentalists. The difference is not one of degree, but of kind. The environmentalist is more optimistic; he considers the problems in his field can be fixed without changing the social framework. William Tucker belongs to this school:

> What is needed now is a fresh approach which sees environmental problems basically as economic problems which tell us not that we are living at the end of the world but only that we are doing a few things wrong which need to be corrected. Environmental problems must be approached in the spirit that they are solvable, and not that they are messages which convey the malignant intent of an evil business establishment, or the first reckoning of domesday. A new pragmatic, optimistic approach to environmental problems would be the best possible legacy of the Age of Environmentalism. (6)

These optimistic words of 1981 sound hollow in the aftermath of Chernobyl. In the field of environmental control, palliatives are no longer enough. Yet the environmentalist approach continues to be adopted by many scholars who are deeply concerned. One of these is Norman Meyers, who deplores the loss of tropical moist forests in terms of its repercussions on many activities: genetic plant material that would be lost to modern agriculture, the campaign against cancer which would be set back for years. Above all he deplores the loss to technology for the tropical forests which store solar energy and could generate vast amounts of energy in the forms of methanol and other fuels to help solve the world's energy crisis. (7)

The term 'deep ecology' was coined by Arne Naess in the early seventies; it is now most widely used by American scholars who have a home-grown tradition of environmental concern. Today, Fritjof Capra considers that deep ecology must explain nature in terms of 'systems theory', to set it well apart from traditional, reductionist science:

> Systems are integrated wholes, whose properties cannot be reduced to those of smaller units. Instead of concentrating on basic building blocks or basic substances, the systems approach emphasizes basic principles of organization. (8)

But Arne Naess has gone deeper than the 'systems' approach:

> The term *deep* is supposed to suggest explication of fundamental presuppositions of valuation as well as of facts and hypotheses. Deep ecology therefore, transcends the limit of any particular science of today, including systems theory and scientific ecology. (9)

Worster offers a philosophical interpretation of the two opposing schools:

> One of the most important ethical issues raised anywhere in the past few decades has been whether nature has an order, a pattern, that we humans are bound to understand and respect and preserve. It is the essential question prompting the environment movement in many countries. Generally, those who have answered 'yes' to the question have also believed that such an order has an intrinsic value, which is to say that not all value comes from humans, that value can exist independently of us. (10)

And Worster thinks the division between the two ecologies will not go away:

> The split between this organic, communal ideal and more pragmatic utilitarianism remains unresolved. In the current 'age of ecology' the ethical-economic debate continues. Our

fundamental task, in this writer's view, is now to choose
between these two moral courses, and thus to decide where
this science of ecology can and should lead us. (11)

Elaborating what he has named 'ecosophy,' Arne Naess
draws on the insights of Eastern, non-linear thinking which
have been lost to the West through excessive reliance on
rational and scientific thought. He insists that such a
philosophy needs to be formulated to form a base for
'fundamental priorities of value'. His starting point is the
distinction between the development of the ego, or narrow
self, and the development of the wider Self, which Naess
spells with a capital 'S'. Self-realization, he contended is
found through the realization of the comprehensive Self, not
through the cultivation of the ego. He sees the widest
connotations of the Self expressed in the Hindu concept of
Atman. This Sanscrit term can be variously translated as
'self' or 'spirit'. The Bhagavadgita contains a verse which
Ghandi translated as: "The man equipped with yoga looks on
all with an impartial eye, seeing 'Atman' in all beings and all
beings in Atman." (12) The same idea is expressed in William
Blake's lines from *Auguries of Innocence*:

To see a world in a grain of sand
And a heaven in a wild flower.
Hold infinity in the palm of your hand
And Eternity in an hour.

Naess has grafted his philosophy with its current of
eastern mysticism onto what was originally a biological
science. The graft has taken.

The word 'ecology' first appeared in Germany in the late
19th century to denote, 'the science of the relations of living
organisms to the external world, their habitat, customs,
energies, parasites, etc'. But the concept already had a long
history in the Western world, where it has perhaps always

been associated with a protest against the separation of man from nature. In the East, as Naess noted, that damaging separation was never enshrined in philosophical or religious doctrine. In the West, the domination of nature by man could draw authority from both the Old and New Testaments, although both books also have a contrary current of teaching which enjoins responsible stewardship of nature.

In the 18th and 19th centuries, the dominant Anglo-Saxon name for ecology was 'nature's economy', a phrase which came to signify a mechanistic analogy between nature and economics. 'Nature is a great economist, for she converts the recreation of one animal to the support of another',wrote Gilbert White, the father of this tradition, in the 18th century. But there was always a softer side; White had inherited from the ancient Greeks the arcadian vision of natural harmony, a notion which flowered in the 19th century in John Buroughs' view of nature as a 'huge organism pulsing with life, real and potential'. Already, conceptions of the natural world were described as wholistic and organic. That view reached its romantic apogee in the United States, in Thoreau's subversive idyll, *Walden's Pond*, the first 'green' polemic of the modern world.

Ecological thought took a more sombre turn when Darwin and Malthus developed the notion of nature as a battleground for survival in an overcrowded world. In the New World, this grim theme had been acted out in the wholesale subjugation of immense virgin territory and the massacre of the native Indians whose ancestors had lived in harmony with that same territory for thousands of years. Here was America's first great ecological dilemma. The ecologist Frederick Clements had developed his seminal theory of the progression of natural systems to a point of mature stability, which he called 'climax.' But the westward-moving pioneers and settlers were systematically destroying that stability, as Worster records:

The two processes of development were fated to meet. One would have to give way to the other; it was not possible to have both a climax state of vegetation and a highly developed human culture on the same territory. (13)

That dilemma has never been resolved. Mainstream ecology has become marked by the mechanistic model of society. Much recent and even contemporary ecology treats nature as an extension of economics—as a reflection of the modern corporate, industrial system as Worster complains. Wholism has been discredited; reductionism brought back. Even among ecologists who are not reductionist in approach there is a trend which the deep ecologists abhor, leading to a return of the grim Malthusian 'lifeboat ethic'. This identifies the most pressing problem of the environment as population growth. In this spirit the neo-Malthusian biologist, Garret Hardin, argues that over-population will exceed the 'carrying capacity' of the earth. He takes as an allegory the ancient tradition of 'the commons', the village land available for all to share. It only requires the selfishness of one individual, who adds one extra cow to the hundred that the land can support, to spoil the commons for everyone. As a consequence, restricted access to common land and private ownership (as 'stewardship') are justified. (14) But Hardin is too pessimistic and his allegory of the commons displays ignorance of history and anthropology. In the medieval period strip farming and common land were managed for generations by peasants through customary law and the power of tradition. In modern times education and information can inform people where their best interests lie.

Hardin, in another equally unpleasant allegory, insists that ten men in a lifeboat must push out the eleventh, as there is only enough provision for the ten. This argument is sometimes transposed as a rationalisation that we should not give food aid to over-populated third world countries because the planet lacks resources for all. Such views justified the

'Environment Fund', which was launched with Hardin's support in 1977 and the Zero Population Growth Movement, which sought population control by repressive measures where necessary.

Today, the more influential deep ecologists dismiss the notion of an absolute 'carrying capacity'. Their aim is a sustainable and healthy society, free from the pressure that causes populations to explode, pressure caused by too rapid economic development and industrialisation. One answer to the lifeboat ethic might be that if the ten men helped their drowning fellows they might come across a shoal of fish, much easier to catch with more hands available. Hardin and other 'scientific' ecologists complain that non-scientific arguments are subjective and value-laden. But what is so wrong with using non-scientific arguments? Science itself is a value and its concepts continually impose values.

Another answer lies in realizing that the teeming millions do not consume the world's resources, whether they are renewable or not; it is the industrialised people who do so. An American baby consumes sixty times more energy than her Indian counterpart; an American housewife uses the energy of five hundred slaves working the year round—and the rest of the over-developed world does not lag far behind. Rich-world communities of the temperate zones, containing one-fifth of earth' s population, account for four-fifths of raw materials traded through international markets.

Reacting against neo-Malthusians, whom he associates with 'eco fascists', the deep ecologist Murray Bookchin argues:

> To use ecological dislocations as a means for reverting to an 'ethics' of crass egotism, to build a 'strategy' of self sustenance on the myth of a stingy nature that faces depletion of its bounty, to elicit a meanness of spirit in the presumption of 'scarcity' is an horrendous mockery of ethics, nature and even the traditional concept of scarcity as a

stimulus to progress. (15)

Some critics of contemporary ecological thought complain of a repressive, even fascist strain. Dissecting the movement from a Socialist viewpoint, David Pepper objects when the *Blueprint for Survival*, drawn up by *The Ecologist* magazine in 1972, calls for legislation and the operation of police forces and the courts to enforce responsible ecological behaviour. Pepper lists this and other aspects of ecological doctrine as 'the unacceptable face of ecotopia'. (16)

Pepper is justified in objecting to a deeply conservative strand in some ecological thinking, especially the tendency to hark back to a mythical golden age of total stability, which generally implies a degree of conformity, constraint and authority, unacceptable today.

Deep ecologists are today in the forefront of protest against the increasing authoritarianism of our growth-oriented societies. If an elitist strand in ecology was ever prominent, it is no longer so and, indeed, Pepper's own story ends relatively happily because finally he detects an 'apparent leftward drift' among modern ecologists and environmentalists which is especially marked among the West German Greens.

THE GAIA HYPOTHESIS

The 'age of ecology', usually dated from the appearance of Rachel Carson's *Silent Spring* in 1962, has reached maturity. It is sometimes known today as the 'age of Gaia' because no vision appeals more to the imagination than that of the Gaia Hypothesis, elaborated by the British geochemist, James Lovelock and his friend and colleague, the American micro-biologist Lynn Margulies. In early Greek mythology Gaia was the first goddess:

> Gaia first existed in the Void. Free of birth or destruction, of
> time or space of form or condition, is the Void. From the
> eternal Void, Gaia danced forth and rolled herself into a
> spinning ball. The earth mother created life on her body and
> cherished it. Gaia was revered by her mortal children,
> sustained them in life and received their bodies back into
> herself in their death. (17)

This creation story follows a similar sequence of events to that of *Genesis* and other creation myths, but it is a gentler version. Further, the earth was a self-created organism; there was no patriarchal father figure. Men in the Gaia myth are not on earth to dominate other creatures as they are in *Genesis*. Lovelock and Margulies were led to the conclusion that the earth behaves like a living organism after their studies of the way in which the biosphere appears to regulate its temperature on the surface of the earth and the way in which the oxygen composition of the atmosphere has not varied from between fifteen per cent and twenty-five per cent for billions of years. A steady temperature and oxygen are essential for life; in maintaining both with astonishing consistency, the earth resembles living organisms to the point where it could be considered to be alive.

> We defined Gaia as a complex entity involving the earth's
> biosphere, atmosphere, oceans, and soil, the totality
> constituting a 'feedback' or 'cybernetic' system which seeks
> an optimal physical and chemical environment for life on this
> planet. Gaia remains a hypothesis, but much evidence
> suggests that many elements of this system act as the
> hypothesis predicts. (18)

The observations and calculations in the elaboration of the Gaia hypothesis made use of conventional scientific methods, hence the hypothesis is taken seriously by the scientific establishment, although it remains to be 'proved'.

Whether the hypothesis is true or false is of less importance for the ecology movement than for its use as a symbol and as a focus for ideas and action. Its potency is evident in the growing number of books and articles, which use Gaia in their title or in illustrations and photographs showing the whole earth viewed from outer space.

The Gaia hypothesis has already supplied the model for creative thought on the future of mankind. Peter Russell, in *The Awakening Earth*, unites the idea of the earth as a self-regulating living organism with the idea of humans standing on the threshold of evolutionary development. Russell writes in the optimistic tradition of Teilhard de Chardin. He proposes that, 'if humanity were to evolve into a healthy, integrated social super-organism, it would signal the maturation and awakening of the global nervous system'. (19)

WILDERNESS

Wilderness is the most inspiring of the deep ecologists' ideas. By this they mean the non man-made environment necessary for our spiritual health. The experience of wilderness has been described by poets, mystics and philosophers across time and culture. Where the modern wilderness writers derive their sense of urgency is the certainty that wilderness is threatened. Every month, world-wide, an area of forest the size of Wales is felled.

Humans have a vital need for wilderness, wild places, to help us become more mature; but beyond our psychological needs, wilderness is the habitat of other beings which have a right to live and blossom for themselves... Thus on both the grounds of self-realization and biocentric equality, the wilderness issue as public policy decision and re-creative experience assumes great importance from a deep ecology perspective. (20)

In North America a tradition of wilderness has existed since the nineteenth century, grafted upon an earlier native Indian tradition. Thoreau, one of the first exponents of a tradition of wilderness, wrote in 1851:

> When I would recreate myself, I seek the darkest wood, the thickest and most interminable and to the citizen, most dismal, swamp. I enter as a sacred place, a Sanctum sanctorum . . . There is the strength, the marrow, of Nature. In short, all good things are wild and free.

The admiration for wilderness from a deep-ecological perspective has led to renewed respect for primal peoples, hunters and gatherers who experience that awareness of place which more sophisticated people have to strive for and cultivate. Primal societies live within their environment; they adapt to it; they allow everything else to live alongside them; they may live for thousands of years in a particular place without altering it. We, today, feel the loss of these refinements and elegancies. When the Inuit woman shaman sings, she experiences her environment in a way that we cannot:

> The great sea
> Has sent me adrift
> It moves me
> As the weed in a great river
> Earth and the great weather
> move me
> Have carried me away
> And move my inward parts with joy

One of the values which belongs with the idea of wilderness is that of the intrinsic right of other beings to exist apart from human beings. The deep ecologist John Livingston points out that trying to justify the existence of a species in its utilitarian terms as a resource implies a contradiction in terms. It has no justification to exist except its very existence.

> To make any argument, any rational, linear logical argument on behalf of the whooping crane is impossible in our language and it's impossible also within the overarching system of beliefs which we've inherited, because the thing isn't of any value. It's probably worth $1.98 if you were to weigh it out on some scales. But is that the point? Must we marshal logical argument in order to address that which is not logical? The existence of the whooping crane is not logical. (21)

This is a moving statement. But in a world where it is calculated that one million species will have disappeared by the end of the century, can it carry any weight?

BIO-REGIONS

Perhaps the most practical of the deep-ecological ideas now in the ascendant is that of the bioregion. This is any area defined not as an administrative or political unit, but in accordance with its geography and ecology. In this way communities, large or small, can find a new identity and act to promote sustainable agriculture, industry, habitation and recreation.

David Simpson and Jane Lapiner were pioneers of practical bioregionalism when they moved out to the Mattole valley in North California, in the early 1970s. What they found seemed to them to epitomize the fate of the whole earth:

> I looked out of the window, and the same thing was happening here in 1974 as happened in Egypt and Mesopotamia and Sumeria and Greece. And it blew me away. It made me realize that what we're up against is the full force... of the history of civilisation...(22)

What happened in the valley was that in the twenty-year timber boom that followed the Second World War, the loggers had taken ninety-five per cent of the old growth timber. The result was massive erosion.

> There's probably over 100 million tons of soil that is stored currently in the Mattole river, clogging the salmon spawning gravel, filling the rearing pools. Some of our friends here who are men in their seventies and eighties remember when they were kids, there was a rock just above the Mattole Bridge ridge there, and they'd dive off the rock. It was 12 to 15 feet above the surface of the water. It was a nice jump. And none of them could touch the bottom of the pool. The pool was 30 to 35 feet deep. And now, not only is the pool gone — filled in, the rock's gone. So you figure there's 45 feet anyway, 45 to 50 feet of silt in that particular spot in the river channel. So you are talking about a monumental change. I mean you look out here. Look out this window at this broad flood plain. Well, there was a dairy farm there, there were hayfields there, there was riparian forest there. It's gone, man. (23)

David and Jane tried to rear salmon fry in hatcheries, but they soon realised that however successful they were, they could never compensate for the ruined river. Now they are trying to improve the whole watershed. They have created a web of home-grown institutions to carry out the immense job they have taken on. Ecological restoration has become part of the way of life of the Mattole Valley. Residents have expressed some of their feeling for their bioregion in art and have formed a successful dance company made up of professionals and amateurs.

> The dance is about wildness and it has this, you know, about human wildness and the wildness of the land and the wildness of the creatures of the land. Their common core as it were. It has this almost religious depth on the one hand, and yet this kind of raw strength, power and beauty. (24)

We cannot all find our Mattole valley, yet the bioregional idea is relevant anywhere and everywhere. Even cities are in bioregions if the inhabitants only knew. Awareness is the primary need, as the American magazine, *Co-evolution* (Winter, 1981), was affirming by devising the following self-scoring questionnaire. Imagine how much more lightly we could live on the land if we all knew the answers:

1. Trace the water you drink from precipitation to tap.
2. How many days until the moon is full (plus or minus a couple of days).
3. Describe the soil around your home.
4. What were the primary subsistence techniques of the culture(s) that lived in your area before you?
5. Name five edible plants in your bioregion and their season(s) of availability.
6. From what direction do winter storms generally come in your region?
7. Where goes your rubbish go?
8. How long is the growing season where you live?
9. On what day of the year are the shadows shortest where you live?
10. Name five trees in your area. Are any of them native? If you can't name them, describe them.
11. Name five resident and any migratory birds in your area.
12. What is the land use by humans in your bioregion in the last century?
13. What primary geological event/process influenced the land form where you live?
14. What species have become extinct in your area?
15. What are the major plant associations in your area?
16. From where you are reading this, point north.
17. What spring wildflower is consistently the first to bloom in your region?
18. What kinds of rocks and minerals are found in your region?

19. Were the stars out last night?

20. Name some beings (nonhuman) which share your place.

21. Do you celebrate the turning of the summer and winter solstice? If so, how do you celebrate?

22. How many people live next door to you? What are their names?

23. How much petrol do you use a week on average?

24. What energy costs you the most money? What kind of energy is it?,

25. What developed and potential energy resources are in your area?

26. What plans are there for massive development of energy or mineral resources in your region?

27. What is the largest wilderness area in your bioregion?

For most of us awareness of that kind is a remote ideal; yet awareness is the first priority of any ecology. And what follows awareness? There is no greenprint for action because ecology, in all its meanings, is as ambiguous as life itself. Even awareness is not enough to ensure action, unless there is a shift of cultural attitude.

This was shown in the great Dust Bowl catastrophe that overtook the American Great Plains in the 1920s and 1930s. Wholesale erosion following over-cultivation in an unsuitable region ruined a generation of settlers. Before long the causes of the disaster were known. The Federal Commission which reported to the President in 1936 left no doubt that it had been a manmade disaster, produced by misguided efforts to 'impose upon the region a system of agriculture to which the Plains are not adapted'. The commission observed:

Nature has established a balance in the Great Plains by what in human terms would be called the method of trial and error. Then white man has disturbed this balance; he must restore it or devise a new one of his own.

With ominous prophetic overtones for what would later happen in the third world, the committee predicted that unless a proper balance could be found, the land would become a desert and the government would have to cope with a perennial, costly problem of relief and salvage. Many of the correct lessons were learned in the Great Plains and beyond and the disaster helped give the infant art of conservation a more co-ordinated ecological perspective. But without a cultural shift, one problem solved can only erupt elsewhere. The historian of the episode, Donald Worster, concludes:

> At the very root of the abuse of the plains lay not only an ignorance of natural science but more importantly a cluster of traditional American attitudes. According to the committee, these included the assumption that the corporate factory farm was more desirable than a smaller family operation, that markets would expand indefinitely, that the pursuit of self-interest and unregulated competition made for social harmony, that humid-land farming practices could be followed on the plains. There was also the pioneering view that America's vast natural resources could never be exhausted. (25)

Ecology, however deep, cannot transform the prevailing world view. When ecology works as a science, it must include biology, chemistry, cybernetics and the other branches of the prevailing linear, scientific way of reasoning. That sort of ecology can indeed only be understood in such a framework. Once we start to use intuitive and metaphorical language, we lose street credibility. Hence deep ecologists are attempting the nearly impossible: using a linear mode to convince people to believe in an intuitive mode.

There is another difficulty. Even if a new paradigm emerges to replace the linear-scientific one, that may not suffice to change the way we live and act. Perhaps all that will happen, as Morris Berman has warned, is that we replace the image of a clock with the image of a cybernetic computor. If this happens we will still be talking about nature as a machine, even if the machine has gained in complexity. We shall have replaced one set of lites with another and will continue, as Berman warns, to be more interested in our explanations of reality than in reality itself.

The best way forward, as Berman suggests, is to tolerate ambiguity in our world picture, perhaps because the only trustworthy world view is the world itself. (26)

Notes:

(1) Fritjof Capra, *The Turning Point.*

(2) Tobias, *Deep Ecology,* page 257.

(3) *Ecotactics,* Sierra Club Handbook, 1970.

(4) Donald Worster, *Nature's Economy,* page 34.

(5) ibid, page 22.

(6) William Tucker quoted in Pepper, *Roots of Modern Environmentalism,* page 81.

(7) Tobias, op. cit., page 14.

(8) Capra, op.cit., page 286.

(9) Tobias, op.cit., page 458.

(10) Worster, op. cit., page ix.

(11) Worster. op. cit. page 257.

(12) Tobias, op.cit, page.

(13) Worster, op. cit., page 219.

(14) Pepper, op. cit., page 99.

(15) quoted in Pepper, op. cit., page 205.

(16) Pepper, op. cit., page 206-8.

(17) Charlene Spretnak, *Lost Goddesses of Early Greece* Boston. Beacon Press 1981.

(18) *Gaia Atlas,* page 100.

(19) Russell, *The Awakening Earth,* page 211.

(20) Sessions, op. cit.,page 111.

(21) Interview, CBC, *New Ideas in Ecology and Economics.*

(22) Interview, CBC, ibid.

(23) Interview, CBC, ibid.

(24) Interview, CBC, ibid.

(25) Worster, *Nature's Economy.*

(26) Morris Berman. *Resurgence, March/April 1986, Issue 115, page 2.*

CHAPTER NINE

Sustainable Agriculture

Corn: C B Wookey, © Rosemary and Penelope Ellis

Sustainable Agriculture

AGRICULTURE is cited as a success story of modern technology; in many parts of the world fewer people grow more food on less land. As a result, world food production has kept ahead of population growth—and if food has not been distributed evenly enough to feed everyone adequately, that is not the fault of technology but of governments. Everywhere, sprawling cities have been nourished by the produce of ever more productive fields.

But there is a reverse side. As a mechanised, high-technology industry, agriculture is no longer a way of living; it does not provide a livelihood, except for rich farmers and landlords who act in effect like industrialists; villages have lost their function and once rural populations are driven to live divorced from land and from nature. Landscapes have been levelled, shorn of trees and hedgerows, emptied of wildlife as well as people. The quality of food has been sacrificed to quantity and the relentless drive for quantity has produced costly and unmanageable surpluses in industrial countries.

The 'green revolution' in favoured parts of the third world has been dependant on artificial fertilisers, chemical pesticides, hybrid seeds and irrigation, which have produced problems that are only just beginning to be costed. Even in fertile regions, soil has been eroded and impoverished by over-cultivation, water tables have been lowered, streams and rivers contaminated. In the search for ever more specialised hybrid seeds, thousands of natural strains of rice and wheat, nature's reserve against future disease, have been allowed to perish. When the expenditure of non-renewable fossil fuels, the cost of subsidies, transport and the storage of surpluses are taken into account, modern agriculture is seen as less efficient as well as less convivial than that of the ancient world.

These drawbacks are now beginning to be recognised. People demand more wholesome food, more people want to live on the land and subsidies and surpluses have become too costly. Can a sustainable, diversified and truly *economic* agriculture be restored within industrial society? Some remedies can be applied at once. Smaller, more diversified farms and organic farms can be encouraged; rural planning proceedures can be changed; land can be made available to more people; rural areas can be revived by the introduction of appropriate industries and services. But there is a limit to such measures. We cannot have sustainable farming until we again respect nature and are ready to observe nature's laws, bounties and limitations. Then, we shall rediscover that nature has fertilisers, pesticides and insecticides that work better at less cost and without harmful side-effects. Growing food can then become part of wholesome living, full-time or as a hobby, in cities as well as the countryside. Everybody will be able to work with nature instead of seeking to outwit it.

WHAT HAPPENED TO FARMING?

What has happened to agriculture cannot be blamed on farmers, as the experience of Britain shows. Farming used to be a family-based concern. Large landowners have existed for hundreds of years, but generally their land was leased out to tenant farmers, while the landlords kept a home farm for their private consumption and derived the bulk of their income from rents. Farmers, traditionally conservative in their methods, formed the backbone of rural communities. At the end of the eighteenth century eighty-five per cent of Britons still lived on the land and produced most of the country's food. Today, less than three per cent of the population live in rural communities and not all of them produce food. Rural society has been decaying throughout this century, although this pattern has begun to change today as people move from town to country.

The newly urbanized population of the 18th and 19th centuries demanded vast quantities of cheap food. In the late 19th century, it was assumed that a rapidly increasing population would need to be fed on imported food. With enormous potential supplies of raw materials in the colonies, there seemed no need to preserve rural traditions at home. Foreign meat and grain were cheaper, but the social consequences of allowing and encouraging rural society to decline were not clearly understood. Only today are we aware of the paradox of the inflated prices we pay for our 'cheap' food. William Morris, Thomas Hardy and other writers, chronicled and lamented the decay of rural society, which has continued to our own times. But the policy of allowing agriculture to decline was halted. The fear of food shortages developed during the Second World War, when imports dried up and rationing had to be introduced.

After that war, government policy decreed that farming should be supported to prevent further food shortage in times of crisis. The 1947 Agriculture Act was designed to protect the farmer and farm worker, ensure stable food prices and self-sufficiency in food and, as an agreeable spin-off, preserve the rural environment. Subsidies for more and more wheat, milk and beef were further inflated when Britain joined the European Common Market.

In this way agriculture fell victim to the bigger-is-better ideology. Guaranteed prices encouraged overproduction and the farm subsidies threw a heavy burden on the taxpayer. Minimum prices were fixed at slightly below production costs, which were rising every year. This in effect meant that farmers, despite subsidies, had to produce more and more to maintain their incomes. That was how British agriculture became one of the most 'efficient' and 'cost-effective' systems of farming in the world, although the apparent success rested all the while on the availability of cheap oil to drive the machines.

The combination of technology—tractors, combine harvesters, chemical fertilisers, pesticides and mechanical irrigation—and subsidised prices led many farmers to concentrate on monoculture at the expense of the traditional mixed arable and livestock farming. Vaccines, antibiotics, growth stimulators and intensive rearing practices transformed animal husbandry. And yet, although the farmer now looked like an entrepreneur, he was less of a free agent than before: "The large scale farmer is the middle link of a mega-chain and is no more a free agent than a petrol-station manager or a brewery's publican", Robert Waller writes in *The Agricultural Balance Sheet*.(1)

The effect on the countryside has been dramatic. Over the past decade, some four thousand small farms have been taken over every year by larger units. *The Planet Gaia Atlas* gives these figures for Britain's vanishing countryside.

Every year, 3,200 km of hedgegrow and almost 75,000 ha of heathland disappear with all the plants and animals they support. In just over 40 year 224,000 km of hedgegrows have been torn out, and half the long-established deciduous woodlands destroyed. Over 80% of the flower-rich lowland meadows have been ploughed up or built over. Already more than 300 plant species are officially listed as endangered. (2)

Today the tide is turning. The cost to the taxpayer of agricultural support policies in the industrial world has been calculated by the World Bank at more than $40 billion a year. Our 'cheap food' looks cheap no longer. Farmers now feel they have been let down. However, as subsidies fall and marginal land goes out of production, an opportunity arises to encourage farming on a human scale. The opportunity could well be missed, if the land is allowed to go to speculators for 'development' of yet more suburbs.

Industrial agriculture in Europe has done nothing for the third world. The EEC and other industrial countries often subsidise crops sold on world markets and thereby undercut developing countries. The 1986 World Bank Report complained that these countries ability to compete "may be undermined at any time by increased export subsidies on industrial countries' exports". While subsidies kept grain prices high, new markets were created for grain substitutes like cassava, corn-gluten-feed and citrus pellets. The agriculture of the developing world is often distorted to produce this sort of crop for the rich countries' cattle instead of producing grain for themselves. That is one of the 'hidden costs' of our agriculture; we feed imported grain or grain substitutes to cattle which could have been used to feed the poor of the exporting country.

THE ENERGY FACTOR

Our technical mastery of agriculture depends on great quantities of energy. While oil was cheap, so were our agricultural costs. That equation has been upset since the 1970s, as Fritjof Capra points out: "While American farmers were able to triple their corn yields per acre and at the same time, cut their labour by two thirds, the amount of energy used to produce one acre of corn increased fourfold".

Because of increasing use of pesticides sixty per cent of

food costs are petroleum costs. British farmers use three per cent of national energy consumption on their farms, but a further ten per cent is used in the transport, packaging and processing of their output from the farm to the consumer's plate. The energy used on farms to provide the average protein consumption for each person in Britain in 1972, amounts to nearly a quarter of a ton of oil. When the hidden costs are brought into the open, modern agriculture appears less efficient than that of the ancient world. A Sumerian farmer fed fifteen people and used no machinery beyond a sickle. That, it has been calculated, was twenty times as efficient as the modern farmer when his machinery and fuel costs have been counted.

THE EROSION FACTOR

The ancient farmer was also more efficient in his conservation of his land. Soil erosion is a global problem but people are only recently becoming aware that it is a problem for temperate as well as tropical zones. David Hodges drew attention to the problem in *The Soil Association Quarterly* (1984).

> In Britain we are clearly entering a phase where the interaction between modern agriculture and the soil is becoming critical... There has been a steady reduction in the resilience of soils over recent years, and this a decrease in their ability to withstand the stresses that are placed upon them by food production... [Farming practices responsible for this include]... working the land up and down the slope; removing field boundaries; using heavy machinery which compacts and thereby damages the soil; having the land under continuous arable crops; ploughing up pasture for crops; increasing the area of land irrigated; maintaining bare soil between trees or soft fruit bushes.

All of these practices are common in conventional mechanised farming. Laurence Woodward, chairperson of the Soil Association and Director of the Elm Park Research Station into organic agriculture, told us of his concern for erosion in Britain:

> We're fortunate in having very resilient soils. It's only in the last few years that evidence of erosion is beginning to be accumulated in Britain. That evidence is actually quite alarming. Erosion is largely through water and is caused on fields growing the same crop year after year, with the same rooting systems, being exposed continually to heavy rains throughout the winter.

THE POISON FACTOR

The list of hidden costs of modern agriculture must include the poisonous effect of chemical fertilisers, herbicides and pesticides. These increase yields per acre, but they also poison the soil, the water and the consumer, as Friends of the Earth report:

> It is now impossible to get away from pesticides, 97-99% of all our vegetables and cereals are sprayed with one or more pesticides. *(Soil Association Quarterly 1984.)*

Nitrate used in chemical fertilisers is leached through the soil and contaminates the water table. The EEC limit for nitrate in drinking water is 50 milligrams per litre. The concentration in East Anglian water has often exceeded that, peaking at one hundred milligrams. Brian Crowl recently reported on Radio Four that no sample had exceeded one hundred milligrams and ninety-seven—ninety-eight has come through the taps only for a short period. He added: "We don't normally inform the consumers. We inform the medical authorities". Chemical industries are large, powerful and important. Governments listen to ICI, so do the farmers. Fritjof Capra draws a parallel between the influence of petrol on agriculture and on health:

> As the pharmaceutical industry has conditioned doctors to believe that the human body needs continual medical supervision and drug treatment to stay healthy, so the petrochemical industry has made farmers believe that soil needs massive infusions of chemicals supervised by agricultural scientists and technicians, to remain productive. In both cases these practices have seriously disrupted the natural balance of the living system and has generated numerous diseases. Moreover the two systems are directly connected, since any imbalance in the soil will affect the food that grows in it and thus the health of the people who eat the food. (3)

Products widely used in livestock husbandry include growth stimulators, hormones, antibiotics and vaccines to produce heavier, leaner and faster-maturing animals. There are objections to these methods on humane and medical grounds and there is also evidence that these pharmaceutical products are harmful to humans. Most people can taste the difference between intensively reared and more naturally reared poultry. A growing number of people object to the factory-farming methods used to rear these animals.

THE ORGANIC APPROACH

Organic farming is the best way to a sustainable and human-scale agriculture. The International Federation of Organic Agriculture Movements established a set of standards in 1981, which show that organic farming arises from a philosophical as well as a practical basis. The aims are:

To work as much as possible within a closed system and to

draw upon local resources; to maintain the long term fertility
of soils; to avoid all forms of pollution that may result from
agricultural techniques; to produce food stuffs of high
nutritional quality and sufficient quantity; to reduce the use
of fossil energy in agricultural practice to a minimum; to give
livestock conditions of life that conform to their physiological
needs and to humanitarian principles; to make it possible for
agricultural producers to earn a living through their work and
develop their potentialities as human beings; to use and
develop appropriate technology based on an understanding of
biological systems; to use decentralised systems for processing
distributing and marketing of products; to create a system
which is aesthetically pleasing to both those within and
outside the system; to maintain and preserve wildlife and
their habitats.(4)

These principles involve a return to good husbandry and
to farming as a way of life rather than a part of the industrial
production line. The organic farmer uses composting and
rotations which utilise leys and green manures; he practices
on-farm processing and usually sells at least some produce
direct. What he does not do is use soluble fertilisers, practise
intensive animal husbandry and use antibiotic and hormone
stimulants. These practical techniques and prohibitions are
held together by an underlying concept of a wholistic living
system.

This approach fits in with the ideas of the deep
ecologists, who reject the prevalent fallacy that every
organism has one function, e.g. that wheat produces grain or
sunflowers produce sunflower seed oil. In reality, every
organism is multifunctional, even something we think of as
useless like a weed. Although weeds compete with crops, they
can also provide a home for pests, tempting them away from
crops and when weeds wither and die, they provide green
manure for the soil. That is why the recycling of plant and
animal wastes is so important. Stuart Hill, a Canadian

professor of agriculture, has described a Catch 22 situation on the Canadian prairies where recycling is not possible:

> Grain is exported from the west to the east to feed animals. But the animal manure does not make the return journey, with the result that the western soil is being impoverished and in the east the water is being polluted by the insertion of animal wastes. This is one of the problems of large scale structures—it is much harder to keep the cycles going. (5)

At Elm Park Farm Research Station, one of the few places where research in organic methods continues, Lawrence Woodward explained: "organic agriculture recognizes that everything affects everything else and that one component cannot be taken out of the system without positively or adversely affecting other things". We asked him why we need research into farming that has been practised for centuries:

> It is a return to basic sound husbandry principles; but even when a farmer is using traditional rotations, the techniques that should be available to him have to be developed as different machineries, different varieties are available, as we know more about how to handle manure for example. Take the situation in the East Anglian wheat country today: the farm has become so specialised, that it's actually impossible to expect to return to the old ways of doing things, so we are increasingly concerned as to how we can bring farms like that into balance. That certainly isn't looking back—it's trying to find new developments.

We wanted to know whether a return to smaller sized family farms could be feasible:

> The question of size is very difficult. Speaking personally, I think organised farming works best with relatively

small units: that doesn't necessarily mean the ownership has to change: but you need units of labour and equipment to a certain size...My view is based on the fact that in organic farming the timing of cultivations is crucial: far too often people are on the land before they should and still on it after they should be, simply because of the large acreages they have to plough. Now the damage that does to soil structure is critical in organic farming, hence my view that we need optimum blocs.

There are no accurate data on the number of organic farmers in Europe. Woodward calculates that they probably number less than one per cent of the total. He estimates about five hundred for Britain including some semi-organic farmers. The numbers seem certain to rise, because of the growing demand for organic produce, which has been monitored by the Soil Association. He spoke of a regional survey of five hundred people in 1985: sixty-four per cent said they would pay more for organic food; most would pay up to ten per cent more.

We asked Woodward if he thought there could be a substantial movement of people from towns to the countryside and living in such a way to include growing part of their food on a part-time basis.

In some parts of the country with some people, yes. I doubt if people in the towns would want to come and live in the country and work on farms. Would the farmers want them anyway? Part-time farming and all that—it happened with the organic producers who went to Wales: the only farms they could afford were marginal farms in Wales. There is a community in a broad sense in Wales where people have done that. Because of the lack of economic support they have been forced to try and imitate the existing marketing structures, the move for vegetables into supermarkets.

Organic farming can be big business. We visited one of the largest organic farmers in Britain, Barry Wookey at The Manor, Rushall, Wiltshire. He began farming conventionally, on the large mixed farm he inherited. We found a small, thatched, grey manor house with an well-groomed garden. The drawing room has an understated elegance and comfort, rather like Wookey himself. His manner is brusque, perhaps shy but with a sharp hint of impatience, suggesting a surfeit of ignorant visitors. He is in no sense an alternative person: if he has a vision or mission, these are confined strictly to the field of organic growing and do not include any social changes. A new tax structure to encourage redistribution of land? "I'm not an accountant", he said. When we visit the farm it is clear that he is a farmer of outstanding talent. It is rare to find an estate so impeccably maintained.

Wookey farms one thousand six hundred and fifty acres organically. The large neighbouring farms are conventionally farmed, including that of Wookey's own son. This organic farm employs no more labour than a non-organic farm: sixteen people, most of them working away from the fields. There is a manager, a miller/baker, six assorted helpers, including the miller's wife and a part-time pensioner cutting grass, and eight tractor-drivers. The farm is divided between wheat and oat crops, roots, short and long ley and rough grazing. Stock comprises cattle, sheep and horses. The farm yard would have ressembled the mixed arable farm of old, had there been hens or a cock crowing on a dung heap. The most striking sight are the wheat fields. In mid-August, with the harvest just beginning, could it be possible that a thirty-acre field of standing wheat should show not the least sign of weeds? A neighbouring wheat field, non-organically farmed, showed patches of green weeds: "where the crop sprayer missed out", explained Wookey. His own fields were uniformly clean, with uncut grass verges to encourage butterflies.

Wookey is still establishing his eight-year rotation. He started farming in 1948 and took over Rushall in 1964—and had soon became convinced of the need for change.

Nineteen forty eight coincided with the time chemicals were being introduced and I'd just started farming. All through the 1950s, we were using more and more chemicals. In those same years, we were building up our partridge population—or so I thought—until I saw them almost disappear. That was the first thing that alerted me. Rachel Carson's *Silent Spring* came next and Thalidomide was the third. I thought if a chemical or drug alleged to have got through all the tests could produce tragedies like that—what were we doing with similarly tested 'safe' chemicals on the land? The parallel was too close to be comfortable. I felt that we were playing with fire with those chemicals that we were using; more and more every year and more and more powerful ones every year. I decided to see whether it was possible to farm organically in the modern context.

My first teachers were the old people on the farm, who all grew up with horses and all of them had farmed organically because there was no other way. I picked up a bit here and a bit there—but basically it was just sound farming practice—good husbandry. They don't teach the rules of good husbandry any more. They rely on chemicals instead. I lost money at first on organic farming and I would not advise a young farmer to go organic; it is too expensive. Present day conventional farming is supported by the taxpayer's money. But eventually the taxpayers will get bored with paying to produce these huge surpluses and will want their money to be used in other directions—one of those directions will be towards organic farming. At the moment there is no support whatever from the government for organic farmers, no research and developement, no subsidies and no incentives; there is nothing like the £184 an acre that the conventional farmer would get if he sold his wheat into intervention. So much money is being spent on conventional farmers where it is not wanted that sooner or later the general public will force the government to change direction. Not only for economic reasons but because they feel that the product is better.

The organic farm of John Leyland and his father in Essex is more typical, because it is much smaller than Wookey's. Their mixed farm is a family business on a human-scale, with two hundred and fifty acres of arable cropping, one hundred and fifty grass and some woodland. The Leylands, who don't enjoy talking theory and principles, are representative of farmers who are finding their way back from the new orthodoxies of high-input chemical farming towards a low-input farming which follows many of the old orthodoxies of good husbandry. In the avenue between the two farms, Marsh farm and Bluegates, the Leylands have planted limes between the old crabapples, a plantation for the enjoyment of future generations. We found the Limousin cattle in their winter quarters, enormous brown beasts with an air of pedigreed indifference. One cow about to calve was separated from the herd and waited alone in a stable. Another heifer was stabled with a bull to bring her into season. The Leylands breed their cattle and sheep by non-artificial methods.

My father never thought of turning it into an organic farm. He never thought that it would pay off—he had debts and a family to raise. It's only been in the last five years that the public have become aware of what their food is—so a market has developed and this has transformed the situation. About two years ago, my father acquired the tenancy of Marsh farm that had been down to grass with no inorganic fertilisers on it for ten years. The last owner wasn't organic—he just hadn't bothered—he had lots of land. So we had a chance to have a go at organic farming. There's only 30 acres that could be ploughed here. Now we are in our third year, the first year was oats, last year barley.

The Leylands market through the co-operative of the Organic Farmers and Growers. They reckon that they make a gross profit of £200 an acre, which compares favourably with a conventionally grown crop. Although their yield is only one and a half tons an acre, their inputs are considerably cheaper. Reticent about his principles, John would not admit to having a conservation policy. But he did confess:

The average field size in Essex is 30 acres, ours is 15. We have grubbed out just one hedge in 20 years. We leave our hedges to grow and shade over and we don't spray the bottom of them. We have a fair amount of woodland and we planted up some corners of fields. We never sat down and and said we have to have a conservation policy we just plant some trees and let them get on with it. We will gradually convert more fields to organic as and when the circumstances allow us. If Britain is going to compete with the rest of the world, I think we could compete more effectively organically—by producing at a lower cost. It's my gut feeling. In the next few years farming is going to get very tough because of the EEC and that means that only the most efficient farmers will be able to survive. I think large farmers will survive—even without their subsidy they have the scope to farm more extensively.

John Leyland does not consider organic farming compatible with a vegetarian future. He argues that if this type of farming is to increase, there must be more meat eating, not less.

There would be a lot more grass about and we would need something to eat the grass. There'd be large numbers of livestock around. The pressure would be there. If the price of beef and lamb is too high then organic farms wouldn't be profitable.I feel that we are at least trying to do something about the problems that conventional farmers are in—instead of just sitting back and waiting. They are not getting anywhere really. But it can't catch on round here because there are no longer any animals around.

Lawrence Woodward agrees that animal husbandry would be necessary, if large, specialised arable farms are to be converted to organic methods:

We have experiments—looking at things like municipal composting, what kind of legumes can be grown economically in that situation, the use of green manures, recycling of straw etc. But what we need is a shift of policy emphasis. Today's over-production has come about by technical development and financial support policies. The emphasis needs to change if we are ever going to bring about sustainable agriculture or in fact do anything about over-production. It should be made financially attractive for the farmer to alter the rotation from cereal cropping to a rotation that protects soil cover—the whole range of things like that.

PERMACULTURE

It can be argued that organic farming does not go far enough in altering the relationship of people with the land. To make a living, the organic grower has to keep constantly looking over his shoulder at the conventional high-input farmer and grower.

Permaculture, i.e. perma-nent, agri-culture, claims to be a system which which is permanent, safe, sustainable and a complete energy system. If a Basic Income scheme (as described in chapter three) were ever to be put into effect, large numbers of people, would be enabled to live in rural and semi-rural areas, growing substantial amounts of their own food. The Permaculture system could become relevant and useful in that context; it exemplifies the principle that farming has to work with, not against, the land. Ecological agriculture has to fulfil certain pre-conditions: it must produce more energy than it consumes; it must not destroy its base, i.e. social environment; it must produce energy for local needs; it must gain its energy on site. Advocates of permaculture belief that this is better achieved by their methods.

The word 'permaculture' was coined by the Australian, Bill Mollison, who now spends his time farming in Australia and propagating these ideas world-wide. Mollison had observed how traditional polycultures use their habitat successfully without degrading it. He was also inspired by the book *One Straw Revolution* by the Japanese farmer, M. Fukuoka, who produces substantial yields, not using any chemicals and with no cultivation and no weeding, allowing plants and animals to fertilize the soil.

Natural eco-systems yield more than ploughed and fenced areas. It was found in Africa, for example, that the meat yield of imported, exotic cattle was only 1/60 of the yield of animals culled from wild indigenous herds.

Natural permaculture sites are forests and lakes, swamps and savannahs but the concepts can be adapted to a city garden or any patch of free land. The system exploits each site so that every element has many functions and every function is converted in many ways. It practises companion planting of trees and plants, in which, for example, one plant attracts bees and another discourages pests. Permaculture utilizes the principle of deep ecology *that every living thing is an end in itself;* it does not need to be justified in terms of human usefulness. The principle justifies intensive gardening and the return of large areas to the wild.

A typical permaculture site is designed to use the natural

lie of the land, the water run off and the soil. A dwelling and its garden are surrounded by concentric, radial zones. Annuals are planted near the house—in Zone One—on the principle of the old kitchen garden. Companion planting is used for plant nutrients and pest contol. There is nothing new in that: gardeners plant nasturtiums with tomatoes. The originality of permaculture lies in the way in which it combines ancient knowledge with modern techniques. Zone Two contains the orchard and the poultry; Zone Three are crops like potatoes, sweetcorn and grain, grown by Fukuoka's 'no-tillage' method. When crops are interplanted and overlap, amazing yields are produced. Furthest from Zone One lies Zone Four, which needs the least attention; it has trees used for fuel, with forage and permanent pasture beneath them. Animals are kept in more than one zone. They are stabled near the house but pastured further off. If the correct number of animals are kept, there will be enough forage year round without growing annual grain crops. Fishponds can be fertilised by onsite produced manures.

Permaculture provides strategies for every situation in which people live: it can make the desert productive, reforest eroded slopes, reclaim derelict or exhausted land; it can make swamps productive and use sewage to produce energy or feed fish or crops. (5) It can be practised in towns. In the Second World War, the garden allotments grew immense amounts of food. Present day cities could produce plenty of food both inside and outside their boundaries. Penny Strange writing about Permaculture in *The Ecologist* described the experience of Gil and Meredeth Freeman in Melbourne who, putting Mollison's ideas into effect in a city environment manage to produce eighty per cent of the food needed for a family of four using three hundred and fifty square metres. (6)

Helen Woodley, who runs a nursery in Leominster, is one of the organizers of the British Permaculture Association. It has two hundred paid-up members. Helen says the multi-functional approach of permaculture can enables large or small farmers to diversify. If a mixed farm with a good slope sets up fish ponds, it will increase its income and provide a habitat for rare water fowl, which in turn are an asset to attract visitors. A mixed farm which diversifies can generate enough income for the farmer's grown children to remain on the farm if they wish.

Robert Hart, another life-long student of permanent planting, has established a small forest garden on his farm in Shropshire as a model for people who only have a small town garden. It is a miniature reproduction of the self-maintaining ecosystem of the natural forest.

There is a contradiction in recommending systems of biological agriculture to the industrial world. These systems depend upon an attitude to the land which we have lost. But the inertia of the accustomed view can be altered. Farmers are beginning to see that organic methods, properly carried out, can produce enough profits. Individuals can protect wild-life habitats. But that is only what Arne Naess calls 'shallow ecology' or environmentalism. We need a new attitude to land—or rather a renewal of one of the oldest manifestations of human culture: namely, respect for the land. This can be found within a scientific framework—the idea of Gaia, the living planet; it can be found in the philosophic and religious idea of wholeness. It can be found in the concept of a sustainable agriculture which does not take from the land more than it gives back. We need to return to this wisdom. At present, the people who respect the earth from which they make a living are the fringe. We should remember that fringes knot fabric together and prevent it from unravelling.

Notes:

(1) Waller, *The Agricultural Balance Sheet.*
(2) *Planet Gaia Atlas.*
(3) Capra, *The Turning Point,* page 272.
(4) Woodward, *The Alternative View,* page 2.
(5) Interview, CBC, *New Ideas in Economics and Ecology.*
(6) Mollison, *Permaculture Two.*

CHAPTER TEN

Sustainable Health

Bicycling, Rodale Press

Sustainable Health

HEALTH IS the ability to realise our full potential; which means much more than the absence of disease and cannot be separated from mental and spiritual wellbeing. In that sense industrial society has left us in poorer health than it found us and continues to damage our health with each decade that passes. It adulterates and irradiates our food, poisons rivers, lakes and trees, frays nerves with noise, hurry and crowds. On a deeper level, we have been deprived of both desire and ability to fend for ourselves and have been turned into consumers in every aspect of our lives: consumers of health, no less than food, clothing, shelter, warmth and culture. We have confused health with medicine and expect doctors to provide us with both.

Competition and the survival of the fittest are among the basic precepts of our education, culture and economic life— as if there could be winners in any competition without losers. The losers are condemned to frustration, loneliness and anger, the perfect base for ill health. Even the winners pay the price of stress and its related conditions. And in depriving us of our convivial communities, industrial society has condemned us to separateness. The old are condemned to lives of loneliness and chronic ill health; the handicapped are relegated to second-class status.

Changing our mindset about health is more difficult than about economics or education, because no aspect of science-based progress has greater prestige or appears more indispensible, than modern medicine. In no field of modern activity is it easier to assume that because technology has been good and continues to improve, then the more we have the better. This assumption has held sway in industrial and third world countries alike. And yet in both sections of the world, the assumption needs to be questioned. Is modern medicine really giving us health, or is it merely creating more and more patients? That happens after all with roads: to ease congestion, you build a new or a wider road and in a short time, the new facility attracts additional traffic that fills it up once more. Such a process would be a natural result of treating health as a commodity that is sold or distributed by official services. Thanks to modern hygiene and drugs, we no longer die of childhood diseases, measles or pneumonia; we are survivors, but are we healthier than our forbears or have we subsituted new ailments for old?

An official British report on health inequalities concluded in 1982, that although the rich countries have been spending an ever-increasing percentage of their national income on health services, they have been unable to demonstrate satisfactorily to themselves that much higher spending is clearly related to much better health. (1)

In Britain, supposedly a welfare state, the inequalities of health between social classes have widened further since *The Black Report* was published. Statistical evidence published in 1986. (*The Guardian* 30/7/86) shows how far inequality has increased since *The Black Report.* In 1972, the death rate for semi-skilled and unskilled workers aged twenty-five to forty-four was ninety per cent above that of their professional and managerial equivalents. But by 1982, the excess had increased to almost one hundred and twenty per cent. Put crudely, the poor got sicker and died younger. (2) Although in the immediate terms, these inequalities were blamed on Conservative economic policies, in the long term, they show us that industrial society can no longer redeem its promises. There are not enough goods and services (including health) available for everyone.

People live longer (the rich live the longest), but there is no evidence that when non-fatal disorders and, above all, mental illness are taken into account, they are healthier let alone happier. How can we measure the long-term effects of eating junk food, of polluted water, contaminated vegetables? What is the toll taken by modern complaints that are labelled stress? Modern medicine has some remarkable cures for deficiency states, like beri-beri, rickets, scurvy and from infections which used regularly to kill, like tuberculosis, pneumonia and syphilis. Our surgery can remove gall-stones, mend limbs and replace hips and even hearts. But for many of the commonest diseases there is no effective cure. Medicine can only control and ameliorate the symptoms of: diabetes, epilepsy, psoriasis, asthma, rheumatoid arthritis, chronic bronchitis, Parkinson's disease, depressive illness, irritable bowel syndrome, premenstrual tension, chronic backache, disseminated sclerosis. These are all highly distressing and not a single genuine cure for any of them. Nor have we a cure for loneliness. Hospital wards are crowded with old people suffering from old age. They are in hospital because our society has no other place for them.

The successes of medicine are not necessarily irreversible. Professor Rene Dubus of Rockefeller University pointed out in 1959 that in many respects the Americans of the 1950s were less healthy than their fathers and that Americans were actually dying younger than they had been a decade earlier. He was writing after many years of spectacular progress with new wonder drugs: cortisones and steroid derivatives for arthritis and related disorders and a series of new immunisations. (3)

Thirty million Americans suffer from crippling arthritis,

ten million require treatment for mental illness, one million die annually from heart disease and a thousand die every day from cancer. From these figures, Dr Paavo Ariola concludes, in *New Realities*, that "although we have more doctors, more dentists, more and better-equipped hospitals, better drugs and a greater supply of food than any other nations we are still, by far, the sickest nation in the world".

The same scepticism is appropriate in the third world. Better sanitation and drugs have enabled millions of babies and children to survive, yet modern medicine and the development process that goes hand-in-hand with it, have not given the survivors health. Mira Shiva, a co-ordinator of India's Voluntary Health Association, was giving no isolated view when she told the 1985 TOES meeting that before Western influence, the Indian subcontinent had a sophisticated system of accessible primary health care. This was then 'marginalised' by the introduction of Western medicine until, "with the total disruption of indigenous peoples' way of life and denial of their support systems, impoverishment and ill health grew". The Indian Council of Medical Research confirmed in 1980 that the imported and inappropriate model of health services is top-heavy, over-centralised, heavily curative in its approach, costly and dependency-creating. (4)

Established medicine is criticised in both rich and poor countries for creating dependency. Just as the industrial revolution deprived people of their own means of subsistence, forcing them to become consumers of the system, so modern health which assumes conventional hospital-orientated attitudes, has created a medicalised dependency and robbed people of the concept of health as something they themselves provide for. The dependency is most apparent among the poor in rich countries. Professor John McKnight of Northwestern University, Illinois presented the argument at the 1985 TOES conference:

Health is basically a condition and not an intervention. The basic 'healthist' misunderstanding is best understood by the modernised poor. Injected, treated, cured, cared, educated and manipulated towards 'compliance,' these people know better than anyone else that these interventions are not the source of their health. Instead, each day their lives are physiologically sickened by their impotence confirmed by their intervenors. They are reduced to being 'health consumers,' the raw material of 'health providers.' (5)

A double-bind situation exists here. People readily assume that they can improve their health by eating better, exercising and avoiding tobacco, alchohol, etc. Yet if they suffer the debilitating effects of a stressful environment, unemployment or poverty, they are often psychologically unable to break this dependency. It seems easier to wait in the doctor's surgery and get some pills.

Health, like every other branch of society, must be seen wholistically. There can be no health of individuals unless their society, and their own relationship with it, is healthy. Fritjof Capra, a systematic exponent of this view, links it with other aspects of wholistic thinking by insisting that the 'systems theory approach' applies as much to medicine as to economics:

Individual organisms interact and communicate with one another by synchronising their rhythms and thus integrating themselves into the larger rhythms of their environment. To be healthy, then, means to be in synchrony with oneself— physically and mentally—and also the surrounding world. When a person is out of synchrony, illness is likely to occur. (6)

Capra links wholistic medicine to the shamanic traditions of non-literate cultures, which emphasise precisely the socio-cultural rather than the physiological aspect of disease.

A Western doctor asked about the causes of an illness will

> talk about bacteria or physiological disorders; a shaman is
> likely to mention competition, jealousy and greed, witches
> and sorcerers, wrongdoing by a member of a patient's family,
> or some other way in which the patient or his kin failed to
> keep the moral order. (7)

Many general practitioners today are able to see the connection between this shamanistic insight and the myriad of psychological and social problems which lie at the root of most so-called illness.

The new economics insists that health, as much as wealth must be built into the accounting systems of nations. The opposite is now the case, with expenditure on doctors, hospitals and drugs counted in the GNP, as though they were benefits. In other words, the sicker we are, the better it is for the health business. The drug industry was expecting to spend £180 million on drug promotion in UK during 1987. (8)

The absence of national health accounting means that nobody counts the true cost of such 'wealth creating' industries as tobacco, armaments, high-tech agriculture that poisons food and water, factories that pollute by smoke, water-bourne emissions and noise, business locations that force people to commute over large distances. Nobody counts the stress-costs that fill hospitals.

Official health services are failing to cope with stress-related illness. Doctors do not have enough time to listen, hospitals are short of funds to provide care, social services are cut back. As a result, dissatisfaction with these services has become widespread in the major industrial countries, where more and more people are turning to alternative or complementary medicine. In Britain, well over a million people now consult more than thirty thousand alternative practitioners in a year. Part of the trend is due to the "growing nervousness of the side effects of drugs used in conventional medicine", according to the Director of the Institute for Complementary Medicine, Dr. Anthony Daird. (9)

The disastrous side-effects of some drugs are already well known. There are numerous documented cases of drugs causing serious and even fatal conditions. In the summer of 1986, following the United States' example, junior aspirin was withdrawn from sale. The disease for which aspirin was blamed was the rare Reye's syndrome (around fifty cases a year) which is fatal in about half the cases. But in a Department of Health study of factors causing this disease some strange facts emerged. A quarter of all UK cases lived in rural areas (compared wth ten per cent of all children under fifteen). A surprisingly high number had been exposed to pesticides from crop spraying. Andrew Veitch suggested in *The Guardian*: "No one is offering an explanation, but some of the wisest money is on a combination of factors: a body infected by viruses, perhaps weakened by some genetic susceptibility, is exposed to an environmental pollutant such as pesticides and is finished off by aspirin". (10)

'Bigger and stronger babies, too', claimed a Grant Chemical Company advertisement in 1957. Thousands of childless women were tempted to use the advertised drug, DES (diethyl stilboestral), to improve their fertility and prevent a miscarriage. Years later, many of the apparently healthy babies and mothers developed cancer. (11)

It is well enough known that tobacco is a major cause of cancer. Yet the profits made by multi-national companies and the taxes collected by governments, ensure that this substance is freely sold across the counter without medical prescription. Smoking is on the decline in the industrial world, but in the third world it is on the increase. The Royal College of Physicians reported in 1983 that one smoker in four would be killed by smoking and that on average a smoker of twenty cigarettes a day would lose an average of five or six years of life.(12)

WHOLISTIC MEDICINE

Practitioners of wholistic medicine claim that by adopting their approach to health, our need for stimulants and narcotics will be curtailed because of reduced stress. Ruth Inglis and Brian West, in their comprehensive *Alternative Health Guide*, found three factors influencing the growing trend towards non-conventional medicine on both sides of the Atlantic in the last two decades: Eastern influences brought in by Maharishi Mahesh Yoga; the 'counter-culture of the Sixties'; and research by clinical psychologists, which reinforces the mind-body connection with illness. On a more theoretical level, the Institute for Complementary Medicine explains that the philosophy of natural therapies depends on an appreciation of what it calls life energies. It sees man as consisting of three elements: the physical body; mind and emotions; and vitality or spirit.

When the interrelation between these three is correct, energy flows and good health results... The natural therapies attempt, by individual methods, to restore the natural flow of life energy by removing the causes of these problems. The practitioner's ability to understand the conditions of the life energies is therefore crucial to the success of the treatment. This implies a means of diagnosis that is based on perception as well as usual sight and questioning. (13)

Capra points to the similarity of this view to that of the Chinese medical tradition. When homeopaths speak of the 'vital force,' or Reichian therapists about 'bioenergy,' they use these terms in a sense that comes very close to the Chinese concept of ch'i, which Capra defines as "the various patterns of flow and fluctuation in the human organism, as well as the continual exchanges between organism and environment". (14)

This move towards wholism in medicine is not confined

to the homeopaths, osteopaths, acupuncturists and a hundred other types of alternative practitioners. Mainstream doctors, too, have been in revolt against the mechanistic, high-technology, reductionist medicine that seeks to treat parts of the body in isolation. The British Holistic Medical Association was founded in 1984 by Patrick Pietroni, who believes the two approachs should be brought together in practice. Dr Pietroni is in charge of practical experiments on these lines. One is in the crypt at St Marylebone church, where doctors, complementary practitioners and spiritual counsellors will work side by side on the same patients. How can a harassed general practitioner cope with wholistic medicine, which means listening to patients for a much longer time than he can afford? Pietroni advocates educative and supporting groups of volunteers: health workers, doctors and patients, to which GPs could refer suitable patients. "As a GP, I would rather see twelve patients as a group for an hour and a half than spend five minutes with each alone."(15)

We visited Dr. Michael Monk in Essex, where he practises manipulative medicine and acupuncture. Like so many people who are breaking new ground in society, Michael is chary of labels: "There are precious few doctors even within the movement, capable of practising wholistic medicine, they still practise symptomatic medicine."

Dr Monk started his career as a conventionally trained doctor. He became interested in problems of back pain and found conventional medicine limited in its ability to diagnose and treat this problem. He worked part-time as a consultant radiologist in the NHS to finance his own part-time studies in manipulative medicine. For the last seven years he has practised privately with a growing clientele. "I treat a cross section of patients," he told us. "I like it that way. Sometimes a patient can't pay." He shrugged. "I'd still rather treat them."

As an ex-radiologist, one of the things that gave me a great deal of pleasure when I first started—and it still does—is the contrast between using machinery costing an awful lot of money and the approach of just using one's hands to make a diagnosis. For example, I had a patient who'd been in a London teaching hospital for persistant neck pains. He'd been put through every diagnostic procedure they had. The cost was enormous, around £1500, I'd say. They couldn't find the cause. I examined him physically. He had trouble in a joint. After two treatments he was painfree. That was very satisfying, no machinery—just my hands.

Michael Monk reminded us that before the rise of medical schools in the mid-nineteenth century, someone who wanted to be a doctor went and studied with a practising physician:

You were an apprentice, living in the community amongst your patients. You worked with the sort of doctor you wanted to be and he taught you everything that he knew...But because of the pressure to improve standards, hospital-based medicine got to be thought the best and a lot of good stuff got thrown out. That's the sort of stuff that's coming back now with the rise of complementary and alternative medicine. There has been too much reliance on high-tech machinery, x-rays and laboratories for diagnosis. The simple skills are forgotten...On the continent, manipulative and conventional medicine exists side by side.

Michael Monk thinks the ideas of wholistic medicine will spread. "They have to because conventional medicine has a limited activity in dealing with many complaints." He sees himself as a bridge between the old and the new:

I want to achieve a synthesis between orthodox and non-orthodox medicine. It's a bit one way at present. GP's refer patients. Many people ask to be sent to me. I've helped their auntie's backache or something like that. The people most closed are consultants. They need their eyes opened. I am convinced that the fusion between the two different kinds of medicine will come. They are not mutually exclusive. Of course there is a loony fringe on the alternative side, like there is an ultra conservative side for orthodox medicine.

However, the medical profession as a body is still suspicious of complementary medicine, partly through prejudice and the instinct for preservation of a vested interest and partly because much complementary medicine lacks comprehensive scientific vetting. In 1986 the British Medical Association issued a report, the result of three years study, dismissing these techniques as in the main ineffective and in some cases dangerous. Because the BMS had invited no alternative practitioners to join the inquiry team, these practioners refused to give evidence. The BMA's rationale accords with conventional scientific thinking. Dr John Harvard, the BMA's spokesman, explained: "We are not saying it's a load of nonsense, we're saying you can't measure it scientifically. You have to go outside the scientific system to recommend it. We are not prepared to do that". (16)

COMMUNITY CARE

Can we reconcile science-based hygiene and medicine with wholistic approaches on a world-wide basis? Aware of the need for this the World Health Organisation has outlined a strategy for *Health for All by the year 2000*. It urges a much higher priority to health promotion and disease prevention not only by health services but other social agencies, and more emphasis on the role of families and communities in health care.

When communities retain or reassume responsibility for their own health care, excellent results can be produced with a combination of modern hygiene and traditional forms of social caring. In the South Indian State of Kerala, village community health care on traditional lines is responsible for one of the highest levels of life-expectancy, literacy amd utilisation of health services, as well as the lowest levels of infant mortality.

All the wholistic critics of current practices agree that health in the wider sense can only be maintained by what Capra calls 'a dynamic balance between individuals, families and other social groups. . . This kind of health care cannot just be 'provided,' or 'delivered,' it has to be 'practised'. For industrial countries, Capra suggests restrictions on advertising of unhealthy products, health-care 'taxes' on firms that generate health hazards and other measures. (17)

MacNight suggests that all increases in public expenditure on therapeutic medical services should be faced with a 'burden of proof' that such services, "will be more healthful than applying the same budget to the income of the people, their community organisations or an alternative preventitive approach". (18) James Robertson agrees that the most effective health action falls outside the scope of health services. This means action:

> To improve the availability and conditions of work, the nutrition value of easily available foods, housing conditions, the availability of transport, heating in bad weather, money incomes, family and local support networks, a sense of personal social esteem, and the multitude of other factors that help to determine the level of lifestyles and conditions of living. (19)

Conveniently, and ironically, much of this programme is in line with current economic exigencies. In both the industrial and the third worlds financial resources are inadequate to maintain the health 'system.' In the third world, grassroots medicine is growing more popular because of lower costs and the possibility of using locally trained 'barefoot' personnel. In a country like Britain, although we cannot self-help ourselves to health, nevertheless, many health conditions can be prevented and treated by a wholistic approach, in preference to the glamourous, high-tech solutions which benefit only a few. A wholistic approach to medicine involves the use of low-tech solutions. For most heart patients, arteries get furred-up by a combination of bad diet, little exercise and chronic stress reactions. These causes can all be eliminated. We may need professional help and advice, but above all we would need to stop relying upon tobacco, alcohol, caffeine and inactivity. We would need to learn the techniques of relaxation.

HEALTHY EATING

The bridge between a highly technological medical service and a self-help community health service can best be built by paying more attention to the food we eat. Changing food habits and attitudes to food production are that part of wholistic thinking that has gained the widest acceptance in the public mind. Many people who are doubtful about complementary and alternative medicine are ready to favour organically produced and additive-free food. Many people are also developing a conscience about the impact of Western food habits on the third world; the vegetarian movement is growing in influence, allied to, and reinforced by, an awareness of animal rights. David Cornish, senior produce buyer for a large English supermarket, Safeways, explains how the desire for more wholesome food has spread into the general public:

First, there are the people who are generally concerned about the amount of agrochemicals used in the environment. Then there is the health issue. We have had cancer and allergy

clinics thanking us for stocking organics because their
patients develop a severe reaction when they eat ordinary
food...there is what you would call the average shopper who
simply wants to know where the flavour in his food has gone. (20)

Ecological issues and wholistic health creep into the
popular media rather shamefacedly, not sure of their
welcome; healthier eating presents a bolder and more
acceptable face. Brown bread, which used to be a rare and
searched-for commodity in English towns and villages, is now
found in every store even though it is probably pre-packed
and sliced. Sometimes the move towards healthier eating
begins purely by the taste, as in the trend for real ale. The
result is the steady growth of the wholefood movement and
the increasing numbers of vegetarians.

How dangerous the chemicals we eat with our food
really are is still disputed. Dr Jean Monro, whose work on diet
allergy and disease is well-known in Britain and the United
States, has been quoted as saying:

I have no doubt that people die from ingesting pesticide
residues and other chemicals in the food they eat. No, in
scientific terms it has not been proven yet. But we are
beginning to document it. The reactions we see are not just
allergy, but also acute illness and even death. (21)

It seems prudent not to allow chemicals and additives
the benefit of the doubt and to avoid them as much as
possible.

Patrick Pietroni pointed out in his book *Holistic Living*
that our culture has attributed all the healing powers to the
doctor and the illness to the patient. A wholistic approach
involves letting go of this dependent relationship and taking
charge of our own health in all possible ways. The women's
movement has made progress in this direction, demanding a
more human and caring approach in maternity services and

clinics and a return to the midwife/mother relationship, which has been supplanted by the doctor/patient one. Emphasising the part stress plays in the onset of illness, Pietroni shows how quite simple techniques, involving self-awareness, allow us to heal ourselves. These techniques are as much use to us in dying as in living. Death is becoming less of a taboo in industrial society, a trend illustrated by the growth of the hospice movement and a return to the more humane and caring attitude towards the dying.

In the society we want, organised on a human scale, we shall still need our hi-tech hospitals for some illnesses. But most other conditions will be dealt with in our own communities, on the assumption that we cannot have better health unless we are at peace with our human, natural and spiritual environment.

Notes:
(1) *The Black Report*, Penguin,1982.
(2) *Occupational Mortality, The Registrar General, Decennial Supplement for Great Britain*, 1979-80, 1982-83, HMSO. pts. 1 & 2.
(3) Quoted in Inglis and West, *The Alternative Health Guide*.
(4) Ekins, *The Living Economy,* page 29.
(5) Ekins, ibid, page 128.
(6) Capra, *The Turning Point*, page 355.
(7) ibid, page 336.
(8) *The Guardian*.
(9) *The Guardian*, 7/11/84.
(10) *The Guardian*, 11/6/86.
(11) *New Scientist*, 6/11/86.
(12) James Wilkinson, *Tobacco*, page 15.
(13) *Journal of the ICM*, July 1986.
(14) Capra, *The Turning Point*, page 344.
(15) *The Guardian*, 21/11/84.
(16) *The Guardian*, May 1986.
(17) Capra,op. cit.,page 366.
(18) Ekins, *The Living Economy*, page 124.
(19) ibid, page 117.
(20) Erlichman, *Gluttons For Punishment*, page 136.
(21) ibid, page 122.

CHAPTER ELEVEN

The Feminine Principle

Greenham Demo, Graham Turner, The Guardian

The Feminine Principle

THE values of wholistic thinking are interwoven with qualities that are considered feminine. These are called caring, co-operating, thinking intuitively and synthesizing. If we are to have a society with altered perspectives which gives a freer rein to such qualities, we might expect women to be energetically involved in working towards it. But there is not much evidence that they are. They play their due part in green thinking and acting, but they have not been especially prominent. Part of the reason is that many women are involved in gaining equal rights in present-day society. Feminists, fighting to free themselves from false valuations, try to enter the structures of power on equal terms with men. They want to change society from within. While an individual woman may succeed in this, the condition of the mass of women remains unaltered. Indeed, in the third world it may even worsen, as certain kinds of economic development reinforce male power, as we shall see later in this chapter. In addition, a woman who achieves status and power may, without meaning to, adopt prevailing values.

We are dealing with two movements: the woman's movement, concerned with women's liberation in present society and the ecological movement, concerned with the reinstatement of the feminine principle. The latter movement works towards a new society in which the aim of the former movement will be triumphantly fulfilled. Both movements aim to replace this macho, aggressive, competitive society with a more humane, co-operative, wholistic one. These values do not belong exclusively to women, but in our society women are traditionally more adept at expressing them.

Men and women do feel, think and behave in different ways. Are these differences due to physical characteristics or cultural conditioning? Does a women's experience as she passes through the various stages of life, affect her differently from her father, brothers, lovers, husband(s), sons and friends? Does the biological destiny of menstruation and menopause, or the experience of pregnancy and childbirth, alter her perceptions so that men and women are thinking, feeling and acting differently? These are questions for which neither scientific methods traditional lore nor new-age thinking can find wholly satisfactory answers.

Historically women have had a bad press, starting from Eve, whose behaviour in the Garden of Eden so infuriated God and subsequent Church Fathers. Like children, women were denied full rights in man-made society; like children they were considered inferior, but unlike male children they were never supposed to become fully adult. In some parts of the world, they remain so, forever under the tutelage of father, then husband.

The facts of women's subordination across time and culture are not difficult to perceive. We know what has happened; we don't agree as to why. Why have women allowed themselves to become the weaker sex? Why do so many women, in various situations, public or private, subordinate themselves to men? Why, when this book is written together, does the male part of the partnership claim a *jus prima nocte* over the word processor, while the female part cooks supper? What each woman has to decide for herself is the extent to which she is prepared to fight against a cultural conditioning that her role is different from and largely subservient to men's. Wholistic thinkers in common with feminists envisage a society where this subordination will be eliminated by new social structures. In an ecological society, women would undoubtedly have a fairer deal. So they ought to press more energetically for rapid changes towards a more wholistic approach. Why aren't they? One answer is that they are sexually stereotyped.

SEXUAL STEREOTYPING

Take language for a start. Humanity is a bi-sexual term, but starting from God, the Father, down to the head of the household, the masculine pronoun is the norm. *Liberty, Equality and Fraternity* are Mankind's prerogative. Women are invisible, linguistically obliterated even in books of great spiritual significance. Random examples taken off our shelves: reading George Trevelyan's *Vision of the Aquarian Age* or Teillhard de Chardin's *The Future of Man,* you might assume that homo sapiens was a single-sex species. Women don't exist in much of our language, although they are not alone in suffering linguistic discrimination. The way in which we express our thoughts uses a male/female, black/white, North/South polarity, implying a sense of inferiority towards one side. A few modern-minded writers make the effort of dropping the clumsy 'he or she' construction to substitute she when the sense means a person. But a concealed fear of women and of their sexuality remains embedded in language, surfacing in all manner of insults. A man is insulted by being called 'a cunt'; a woman isn't called 'a prick'. The hypocrisy of the jibes used against prostitutes in every culture show up this ambiguous and ambivalent attitude.

In language she is obliterated; in art and popular culture, however, the image of woman is used to represent romantic, sexual, even patriotic themes. Two symbols predominate, the all-providing Earth-mother, from the Virgin Mary to Gaia; and the sentimentalised, accepting 'little woman'. Danger lies in accepting either of these stereotypes. The former can lead to an escapism in which women are identified with nature and absolved from traffic with the real world. In the latter, taken to its extreme, we are reduced to the image of the sanitized deodorized American Mom, creating the beautiful home while Pop brings home the bacon. This image is not out-of-date; you only have to look at the message the advertising media are still putting across, or read the political speeches glorifying the position of 'women in the home'.

Gender stereotyping starts young. If you decide to bring up your little boy to play with dolls and your little girl to play with cars, you had better censor her reading and his too. Can you imagine Jill climbing the beanstalk and vanquishing the giant; or the princess kissing the finger-pricked prince awake; can you see the seven lady dwarves after their day's mining, weeping to find Snow White has eaten his poisoned apple and fallen into a swoon. Does Ulysses weave his tapestry, outwitting his angry, brawling lady-suitors and Penelope sail the wine-dark sea, or is Oberon lulled to sleep by his fairies?

Does sexist education reinforce inherent differences, or do inherent differences force us to educate the sexes differently? Social conditioning operates on different levels for boys and girls even in mixed-sex schools. It has been shown that girls in single-sex schools perform better in science subjects than when boys are present. Broadly speaking, boys take science subjects, girls take the arts. These differences are reflected in university scientific degree results, in which males predominate. Twice as many boys took Physics O'levels as girls in 1986 in Britain. Boys are educated for one career, but girls are assumed to have two. No one suggests educating boys for parenthood. Both sexes are the losers because the feminine side of boys' natures is trained out of them. How rarely we see a man cry, yet there is no biological difference in masculine or feminine tear ducts. Women are still portrayed in the popular media as sexual objects or as mere domestic consumers. Nor do many women reject these images of themselves. Women don't boycott products which are advertised showing them as brainless pretty idiots; they don't object to make-up, however time-consuming to put on and expensive to buy, or high heels, however uncomfortable and unhealthy. The media portray two parallel worlds of which the feminine one is lower down the scale and less important. Women acquiesce in their stereotyped image. Being a housewife and mother is still not considered as an occupation.

FROM MATRIARCHY TO PATRIARCHY

Where in time past, did this sexual imbalance come into being? Some anthropologists claim that in matriarchal societies, women are granted greater respect and a larger role to play. But even in matriarchies, the mother's brother is often the prime authority in the family.

Matriarchy is described as forming a non-violent base for society in Erich Fromm's *The Anatomy of Human Destructiveness*. One of the earliest known centres of civilisation, has been excavated at Gatal Hyk, in Anatolia. The oldest level of this neolithic site has been dated c.6500 BC. Some interesting speculations have been made of this and similar sites. First there was little class distinction between rich and poor; there is no definitive evidence of chieftanship and such social inequalities that are suggested by size of buildings, equipment and burial gifts imply a narrow range of inequalities. In the eight hundred years of history so far explored, there appears to have been no sack or massacre and also in the hundreds of skeletons so far examined, none died a violent death.

Why might this have been so? One of the most

characteristic features of neolithic villages was the central role of the mother in their social structure and religion:

> Following the older division of labor, where men hunted and women gathered roots and vegetables, agriculture was most likely the discovery of women, while animal husbandry was that of men. (Considering the fundamental role of agriculture in the development of civilisation, it is perhaps no exaggeration to state that modern civilisation was founded by women.) The earth's and women's capacity to give birth—a capacity that men lack—quite naturally gave the mother a supreme place in the world of the early agriculturalists. (Only when men could create material things by intellect, i.e. magically and technically—could they claim superiority.) The mother, as goddess (often identified with mother earth) became the supreme goddess of the religious world, while the earthly mother became the center of family and social life. (1)

Children were buried with their mothers not their fathers which is a common trait in matriarchal societies. The central role of the mother goddess can be seen in the statues, wall paintings and reliefs that have been excavated. The mother goddess of neolithic times was also the patroness of the hunt, of agriculture and of plant life. In more historical times she was represented by Cybele, Artemis, Aphrodite and Astarte. Erich Fromm, after studying the archaeological data, favours the view that:

> Neolithic society was relatively, egalitarian, without hierarchy, exploitation, or marked agression...these Neolithic villages in Anatolia, had a matriarchal (matricentric) structure, [adding] a great deal more evidence to the hypothesis that Neolithic society, at least in Anatolia, was an essentially unaggressive and peaceful society. The reason for this lies in the spirit of affirmation of life and lack of destructiveness which J.J.Bachofen believed was an essential trait of all matriarchal societies. (2)

Bachofen's book *Das Mutterrecht*, published in 1861 found little favour with the 19th century intellectual establishment. He wrote: "whereas the paternal principle is inherently restrictive the maternal principle is universal; the paternal principle implies limitation to definate groups but the maternal principle like the life of nature, knows no barriers".(3)

There has been a transition from the matriarchal principle to the patriarchal principle throughout the world apart from a few scattered examples. The degree to which very early agricultural societies were gentle and non-agressive can never be proved. It is of great historical theoretical interest, but it seems unlikely that we are en route to returning to simple agricultural communities. Whether we like it or not, our reforms have to be within the context of industrial society, which will not vanish because some of us dislike it.

We are still living in patriarchal society despite cracks in the facade of male power. Men are demonstrably heavier, faster and better able to lift heavy weights. But what of more subtle less easily quantifiable differences?

FLEXIBLE THINKING

There is evidence that women can use their brains more flexibly than men, which helps explain many observable differences in daily life. Marilyn Ferguson remarks briefly in *The Aquarian Conspiracy:* "women are neurologically more flexible than men" . . . and she continues, "and they have had cultural permission to be more intuitive, sensitive, feeling". What she refers to when she says neurologically more flexible is the surprising discovery that women can use both hemispheres of their brains more easily than men.(4) Physical movement of the left side of the body is controlled by the right hemisphere of the brain and the reverse. But as well as physical co-ordination, the two hemispheres have different functions. The left hemisphere controls linear reasoning, speech and analysis; the right hemisphere controls feeling, initiative, subjective thought, space and synthesis. The right hemisphere recognizes objects in space, images and patterns and it covers our intuitive sense. Artistic creativity is a right hemisphere function. Both hemispheres can function independently of each other but in most people and in most literate cultures, left brain hemisphere thinking predominates.

Julian Jaynes in *The Origin of Consciousness in the Breakdown of the Bicameral Mind* discussed this gender difference with reference to the fact that in the ancient world the oracles and Sibyls were usually women. Speech resides in the left hemisphere, but divination would originate from the right. Therefore individuals who could use the intuitions from their right hemisphere and transfer them into speech with the function of the left, would be able to prophesy. This flexibility was produced in the ancient world more easily by women than men.

It is now well known that women are biologically somewhat less lateralised in brain function than men. This means simply that psychological functions in women are not localised into one or the other hemisphere of the brain to the same degree as in men. Mental abilities in women are more spread over both hemispheres. Even by the age six for example, a boy can recognize objects in his left hand by feel alone better than in his right hand. In girls both hands are equal. This shows that haptic recognition (as it is called) has already been primarily localized in the right hemisphere in boys but not in girls. And it is common knowledge that elderly men with a stroke or haemorrhage in the left hemisphere are more speechless than elderly women with a similiar diagnosis. Accordingly we might expect more residual language function in the right hemisphere of women making

it easier for women to learn to be oracles and indeed the
majority of oracles and Sibyls, at least in European culture,
were women.(5)

That women are in general more sensitive and intuitive
than men has for long been a part of popular lore. Women's
celebrated intuition turns out to be more than her imagination. Men and women often approach problems from
different angles and this now appears too have a physiological
basis. We would argue that the fact that women pass more
easily from the rational mode to the intuitive mode of
thinking enables them to be more readily sympathetic and
caring. This ability to synthesise, think round a subject does
appear to be a gender difference which is not often noticed.

The Chinese talked about the balance between yang
masculine qualitites and yin feminine qualities. This concept
is sometimes equated with left and right brain thinking. In
contemporary society yang qualities of competitiveness, self-
assertion, rational, analytical linear thinking are preferred
over co-operation, intuition, emotion and wholism. In
patriarchal systems, a balance has been lost. One type of
personality and one sex, one way of thinking, becomes
favoured over others to the loss of all. Is a synthesis possible?
Could we allow both sexes to develop their yin and yang
qualities?

That there is a feminine perspective in a given situation
is recognized by many alternative thinkers.

Jonathon Porritt represents much of current green
thinking on this issue. We asked him whether he thought the
Green movement was sufficiently radical over women.
Would women find themselves at the bottom end of the social
pyramid even in a green world? Did he see women at the core
of green thinking?

Yes, in many ways I do, because the whole way we are
seeking to change the process and change attitudes and

policies, my own feeling is that women have access to that kind of more humane, gentle, considered, responses than men do, and that men have been conditioned into a far more brutal concept of what progress and success is than a lot of women have. You have to be terribly careful here because you only have to go a tiny bit further and you can start patronising women as I've often noticed in certain parts of the green movement. You know: women are less competitive and therefore bound to be better, as if to say a woman couldn't actually compete in a male world. Rightly I think Greens are ticked off by the women's movement for a sort of pseudo-feminism. However, I feel very strongly this notion of the destructive impact of materialism and industrialism on the balance of each individual: the feminine and the masculine. Restoring that balance is very tricky. I don't think we can restore it unless women play a stronger role in our society. I wouldn't pretend that the green movement has succeeded with this in this country as well as the green movement in Germany. The Green Party has three co-chairs but nobody knows that, it hasn't made much impact.

WOMEN AND GREEN POLITICS

In the green movement, the most sympathetic political movement to feminine values, the positions high up in the hierarchy are still male-dominated. The subject of women in society is baffling, complex and highly controversial; nobody has really worked it out and Greens are no exception. They pay lip service to the reintroduction of feminine values but their thinking is still dominated by patriarchal values current in society. In drawing some of the parallels between feminist and ecological thinking, we can see that core ideas of the two movements could benefit one another much more than they do already.

The following remarks of Francis Kinsman, co-founder

of The Business Network and a leading exponent of wholistic approach to business, shows both the green sensitivity and also its limitations:

> In short, then, women as a vast untapped resource now realise their own potential, and business is beginning to realise it as well. There has had to be a period of hysterical way-out exaggeration to bring the whole feminist issue to the attention of the public in general and to other women in particular. Without the strident claims of a few viragos, very little would probably have happened and the status quo would have been more or less maintained by the patriarchy of the establishment. But since the storm troopers in the van of the revolution became such a newsworthy pressure group, gradually the great mass of people are moving over to the more comfortably balanced middle position that will characterise opinion in future. (6)

Kinsman admits that without 'a few viragos', nothing much would have changed, although the situation appeared grave enough to warrant the viragos acting as storm troopers. We are not informed what this 'comfortably balanced middle position' is, either. We suspect it will be very like the old status quo with a few token women thrown in to middle management.

'The patriarchy of the establishment' which, as Kinsman acknowledges, maintains the status quo is an institution that feminists have been analysing vigourously for the last twenty years or so. This gives the alliance between feminists and ecologists great strength; both movements wish to shake the foundations of patriarchal society. However, they do not necessarily have the same ultimate aims.

When women wish to enter the public sphere they have to fight against prejudice that is largely unconscious in their male colleagues. The following experiences of two women, Jan Palliser and Dorothea Clift, illustrate how gender difference is perceived in an actual situation when women intrude in public life. Dorothea Clift remembers with mixed feelings the time she spent on an expert and predominantly male, committee. Gradually she realised that the other women, although more experienced than she was in sitting on a prestigious government sponsored committee, also had difficulty in being heard.

> We had a problem, both of the message and the medium. Our message was different from the men's main concern. They enjoyed arguing about professional methods and techniques, swopping statistics... and sharpening their wits by attacking other men's theories and defending their own... The women members were more concerned by the individual lives represented in the statistics that were tossed around. We also wanted to question some of the men's motives; were they really concerned about the hopes and beliefs of their clients or were they guided by paternalism, benevolent or not so benevolent? If they did not listen to us, did they listen attentively to their women clients? *(The Guardian 30/12/86)*

She described the four stereotypes that women in public life are pressed into; the earth mother, the reprimanding nanny or schoolmarm, the bluestocking and the dumb blonde. These stereotypes all refer to children or child care. 'If we are unconsciously seen as children or as children's companions, how could we relate on equal terms with the expert verbal swordsman?' The trouble with stereotyping is that it prevents you from hearing what the person is saying. "I was surprised at how often the men complained that the women talked too much, because I felt that we spoke for only a small part of the time."

Jan Palliser complained in similar vein when she attended the Second Congress of the European Greens in Dover in 1985:

After years of going to women-only meetings and events, the
male-dominated congress came as something of a culture
shock. Throughout the Saturday, male speaker followed male
speaker . . . The sad fact that movements fighting for freedom
and equality still perpetuate inequalities based upon sex is
evidence of the rampant persistence of patriarchy. Patriarchy
means the overall supremacy of the male over the female and
it is this that feminists have been fighting for centuries and
across cultures. And significantly it is patriarchal culture and
thinking which is at the root of indiscriminate growth and
careless industrialism and of war-mongering technologies.
Feminism and ecology should logically therefore go hand in
glove in the fight to overcome patriarchy.

Charlene Spretnak remarked ironically at a
Schumacher lecture that she had been reading all the
critiques of modernity that she could find, most in print were
written by men. She added, "I must also note, however, that
these well-intentioned men never seem to notice, while
rhapsodizing over the need to return the feminine symbol to
our notion of deity, that no flesh-and-blood females have been
invited to speak on their panels, at their conferences, or in
their journals".

The most prominent women's success story among
Greens comes from West Germany. But here too the victory
has been less than decisive. Green women in West Germany
aim to undermine what they call the five thousand year old
patriarchal rule in the West, according to Ms Marieluise
Beck-Oberdorff, a Green deputy in the Bundestag. She was
speaking in a debate on women's unemployment in 1984.

Just imagine if men worked a 12 or 16 hour day on their own
households without pay. Would they talk about men's
unemployment? Of course not. They'd call it overwork.
Women's problem is overwork: yet we're last in the queue for
real jobs, properly paid with proper advancement and proper
pensions at the end.

In 1984, the Greens 'feminat', or female ruling group, was the first in history to run a parliamentary party. One of them, Gaby Potthast, argued that men were parasites in a society where women did two-thirds of the essential work. "Out of 26 million women over 15 in this country, 16 million do not dispose of an income on which they could live. The revolutionary aim is something like a 20 hour week for everyone at 'official' jobs, each sex equally paid and sharing the household chores."

All this goes against the *Kinder, Kirche, Kuche* (children, church and kitchen) emphasis of traditional German virtues, but it has had only a limited impact. Chancellor Kohl was quoted in a election address: "our pretty women are one of this country's natural resources". West German and British Conservatives often argue that unemployment would be cured if only women learned to stay at home.

But women have stopped staying at home, in one of the most significant developments of the women's movement: peace camps and demonstrations in many countries. It is easy to scoff at peace camps that do not prevent the arrival of missiles; demonstrations that yield no more than temporary media coverage. In Great Britain, however, Greenham Common may one day be considered one of the most significant symbolic actions of the twentieth century. The Greenham women have made peace appear as a feminine concept.

Nuclear defence is a masculine concept; the military establishment is virtually a masculine preserve. The principles of deterrence are part of a political viewpoint that has developed from reductionist, linear thinking—a point women appear to have grasped more profoundly than men.

When the suffragettes began their campaign, few thought they would succeed. Does it seem any more likely that a few transitory campsites will shake the might of a superpower disposing of military contracts to greedy hangers-on in the rear? Greenham represents what many women believe to be right and their beliefs are echoed world wide, in American peace camps and marches, in Dutch demonstrations and in Soviet labour camps. Women's Action for Nuclear Disarmament, WAND, founded by Helen Caldicott, has been in the forefront of action in the USA. The political action of these women is not part of a wholistic movement, but it runs parallel with many similar aims.

HOUSEWORK

Housework is not even considered by conventional economists as a part of the gross national product. The World Conference in Nairobi, the culmination of the UN Decade for Women in 1985, recommended that "concrete steps should be taken to quantify the unremunerated contribution of women to food and agricultural production, reproduction and household activities". These were fine words, marking a recognition that women's unpaid contribution did, after all, contribute to the GNP. But a campaign for 'wages for housework' seems to us to be misguided. To bring caring into the money economy would be an admission that love and affection can be measured in money terms. It should be possible to consider work as a part of our life, but not necessarily something which has to be done for money. The answer lies in reinstating the 'feminine' for men as well as women. There are many men who, due both to the rapid rise in unemployment and a more relaxed attitude towards gender behaviour, are now able to admit that they enjoy sharing jobs and staying part-time at home. They should be allowed to do so if they wish. Shared housework, can be accepted, not as a paid activity, nor as drudgery, but as an expression of mutual caring. If housework is to be paid for, what's to be included in the price? If cooking is a service, what about arranging flowers, or making love, or knitting? Do you get overtime and bonuses for work well done? Would the Xs' children who passed their exams so brilliantly earn the househusband a bonus, whilst poor Mrs Y with her dirty curtains and truant children deserves the sack? At present we are a long way in industrial societies, from equalizing gender divisions at home and at work.

Throughout the whole range of social institutions, gender divisions remain pervasive. They can be seen in action in the family, the trade unions, the schools and training schemes. Gender divisions are at work in the system of health care, the media, the social security and the tax systems. Women, the grass roots of party politics, are poorly represented in the upper echelons with one or two notable exceptions. The most celebrated British woman politician, who has so triumphantly surmounted gender difficulties, is not noted for her espousal of feminist causes (or for her green thinking).

Male dominance in the family situation and in the public spheres will vary according to social class and ethnic groups. It forms one of those patterns that is so universal as not to be perceived very easily. If both sexes shared the servicing of the home and the care of young and old, and of the chronically sick and disabled, many or indeed most of these problems would disappear.

WOMEN IN THE THIRD WORLD

Sexual stereotyping diminishes women in the third world as well as the rich world because patriarchal systems are common throughout both. In addition, the process of economic development can serve to depress women's social and economic status even further. Development, in practice, often means that more peasants become landless, a transition from a subsistence to a cash-crop economy, in which women lose their traditional role. Women, who already had low status in a subsistence economy, may find that in this new situation their status is further diminished. Govind Kelkar, a research associate at the Centre for Women's Development in New Delhi, has shown how this happens. (7)

Kelkar finds that the green revolution introduced into India in the 1960s has "brought in its wake the all-India trend of pauperization and marginalization and the increased inequality between the sexes". The shift to technological farming drove women out of the agricultural labour force. The new agrarian technology caused a reduction in labour from that of traditional farming to about one fifth. Kelkar points out that removing women from the work force was not a sign of growing prosperity for them. Women still carry out the manual work of transplanting, weeding, threshing, carrying the produce home and processing the food grains. However in India, women are generally paid about forty to sixty per cent of men's wages. Women toil as they do on the farm, alone with their responsibility of cooking for the family and attending the children. Women's jobs are absolutely essential to the existence of the family and yet tend to be very tedious and time consuming.

Kelkar collected evidence from one area, Hamirpur Ruru, but similar evidence can be found from other communities in developing societies. The difference between a Western woman returning from the factory and cooking the dinner and her Indian sister is one of degree not of kind.

Kelkar stresses that in the subsistence traditional economy women had a more valued and important role. In the new technological economy, men have acquired the right to the new goodies and excluded women. This exclusion is justified by religious and social norms and women themselves concur with it.Their work is ignored as unpaid household work and their contribution to production is regarded as secondary or supplementary to men's contribution. Therefore more money is spent on a male child in terms of food, clothes and schooling as he is seen as a potential earner for his natal family. This breeds in the males superior attitudes as they think of themselves as 'the representatives of a new enlightenment'. Women, therefore tend to accept an inferior status, both at home and in the labour market. This social reproduction of values, which devalues women's work, continues, often buttressed by religious teaching and women are socialised into accepting their dependency on men.

What has happened is that the Green Revolution has reinforced the already low status of women as well as other powerless groups in society. These third world societies are more patriarchal than those of the rich societies in the West. But in them women have doubly lost out because development, while it destroys their traditional base, yields less for them as a group then it does the men. Peasant women are often criticised for being backward looking and traditional; perhaps they have been more far-sighted than was supposed. However, third world women are not mere ciphers, allowing the destruction of their livelihoods without making any protests.

Ecological awareness strikes women for whom the death of trees is not only an aesthetic harm but a matter of survival. The Chipko movement in India is a response by people to the exploitation of common resources for the benefit of a few. "Women in village after village clung to trees throughout the 70s to save them from the axe. Chipko—or hug the tree movement that emerged was India's first major ecology movement with roots in an ancient mode of democratic protest." (8)

Ecological protests like Chipko signify more than a protest against exploitative use of forests; they are a protest against the whole process of Western-inspired development. They are in the same spirit as anti-dam protests. It is women from comparatively backward economies who have come to the forefront in these protests.

A SYNTHESIS

The dominant world view has depended upon male

supremacy and this has led to repression of both sexes. In a slave society, the master is equally as debased as his slave; so in any situation where one person denies the other autonomy, both are losers. Sexual stereotyping, by repressing many female characteristics, equally represses male ones. Where women cannot fight: men cannot cry. We are now aware that women are more easily in touch with their intuitive right brain and are less often dominated by one hemisphere, they nevertheless, as men do, have the abilities that belong to a whole brain.

If we are to achieve a synthesis between yin and yang, we must first get rid of the idea that housework is a nugatory feminine pursuit whilst the real work gets done elsewhere. Housework, caring, leisure, childcare and all those pursuits which are considered a) specifically female and b) less important than paid work, will have to be revalued and de-sexed. This would be greatly helped by everyone adopting a simpler, less consumerist lifestyle. For it is women, who in their role of homemaker and sexual object, have been most coerced into the endless cycle of consuming. Living simply is not just a question of keeping paper bags and making compost; it implies an awareness of what products we are using, what food we are eating, how it was produced and who was helped or exploited by our use.

A San Francisco collective suggested the following criteria for living more simply :

• Does what I own or buy promote activity self reliance and involvement, or does it induce passivity and dependence?

• Are my consumption patterns basically satisfying, or do I buy much that serves no real need?

• How tied is my present job and life style to installment payments maintenance and repair costs and the expectations of others?

• Do I consider the impact of my consumption patterns on other people and on the earth? (9)

Voluntary simplicity is extremely appealing to those still fortunate enough to be threatened with a surfeit. It reads rather bitterly to the unemployed, the marginalised, the poor of the world, who feel our indifference.

Our society has consistently valued competitiveness and self-assertion over co-operation. In the cultural conditioning of the two sexes, men are forced to take competitive dominant role and women, submissive, caring, nuturing roles. Familiar stereotypes find the office manager on the telephone while his pretty secretary makes coffee; the brilliant surgeon, palm outstretched to nurse for the scalpel; and the pilot flirts with the air hostess. Women have acquiesced with these stereotypes. There is a familiar security in learned helplessness. As Dorothy Dinnerstein, an American psychiatrist has written, 'so many people who find the symbiosis oppressive, nevertheless feel frightened and bereft at the thought of living without it".

These are the stereotypes that women need to fight against and wholistic thinking does not yet offer them enough scope. Even in green parties, they have to fight the male-dominated scene before they can make their views felt. In religion itself, women now claim to play a more visible role. How long before they can be fully ordained as priests in those religions that they wish to enter? There is among some wholistic or alternative writing, an idealised view of Woman as the Earth Goddess and as non-violent unconditional loving mother. It remains to be seen whether liberated women will continue to be gentle and non-violent or whether they will adopt the social behaviour of their unliberated male counterparts.

The terrible problems facing us, nuclear power, famine and pollution are not gender specific. However women can justifiably claim to have played a lesser role in producing them. Having nurtured children across time and history, they have developed a built-in awareness of the dangers to their children and their children's children.

We have seen that what ecologists call 'the reinstatement of the feminine principle' is far from being accepted. The liberation that we found in the sexual permissiveness of the 1960s has been tragically curtailed by the AIDS epidemic. Nevertheless, it has made an impact on our attitudes towards sexuality. We are no longer afraid to love one another, to explore varieties of sexual experience. But we still find it necessary to obey the rules set-up by class, race and sex. Within these categories, inequalities remain and in some cases have increased. We believe that the shift towards wholistic thinking will create a less exploitative society for men, women and children. Meanwhile, in this chapter, we have dwelt on the feminist aspects of the women's movement, because until the demands of what Francis Kinsman has called 'a few viragos' are met, women will not play a significant and equal role in forming a new society: they cannot.

Notes:

(1) Fromm, *The Anatomy of Human Destructiveness,* page 155.

(2) Fromm, ibid, page 157.

(3) Quoted in Fromm, ibid, page 159.

(4) Sandra Witelson, 'Sex and the Single Hemisphere', *Science.* 1976, Issue 193, pages 425-427.

(5) Jaynes, *The Origin of Consciousness in the Breakdown of the Bicameral Mind,* page 344.

(6) Kinsman, *The New Agenda,* page 100.

(7) Govind Kelkar, *Tractors against Women Development,* no.3, 1985, pages 18-21.

(8) Vandana Shiva, *Ecology Movements in India, Development,* 1985 (3), page 64.

(9) Elgin, *Voluntary Simplicity,* page 166.

Human-Scale Education

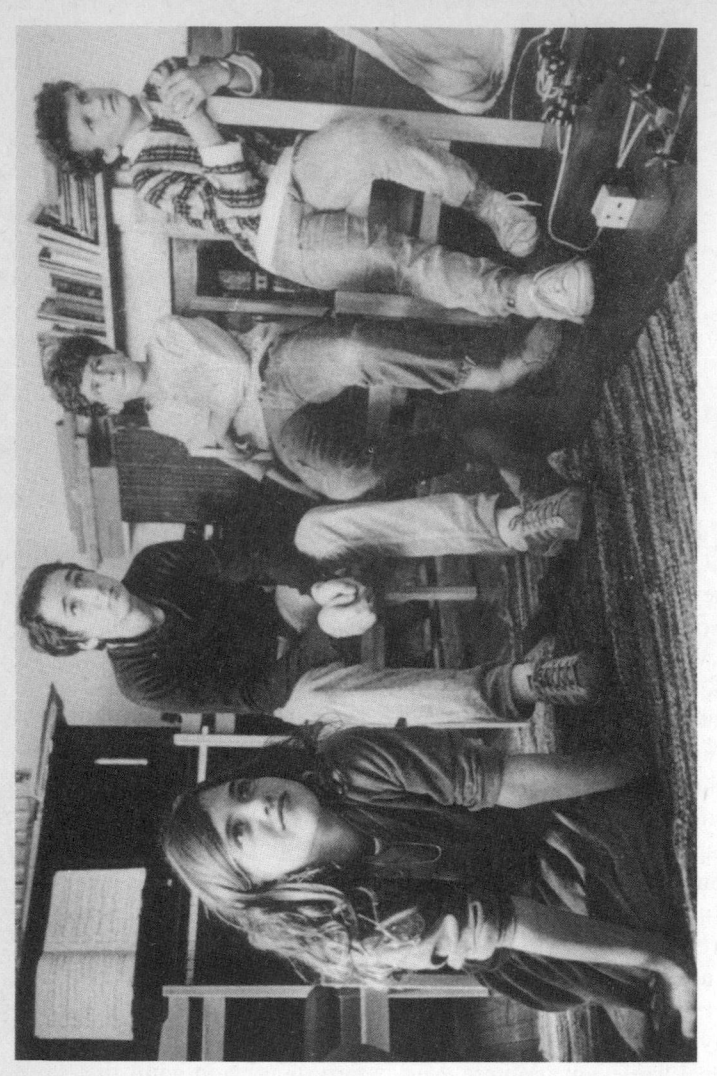

A Music Class at the Small School, Hartland, Devon

Human Scale Education

EDUCATION for what? The old question has never been more urgent. There are three reasons why we need a new type of school:

1. Schools have to teach the prevailing world view, but today, as we saw in earlier chapters, the dominant world view (scientific/materialist/reductionist) is no longer comprehensive. How can schools give pupils a wider view?

2. Industrial society has had full employment as its social base and educated its children with that in view. Now the base is eroded; for many people, full-time, paid jobs are disappearing. In this new situation, what should education be about?

3. In past centuries, schools were for an elite. Most of them were designed as a prelude to universities and they still retain an academic examination structure. Today, schools are for everybody, though only a small minority of pupils go on to university. The result is that the majority of pupils are made to feel irrelevant, failures even before they begin adult life.

What kind of schools? That old question, too, is reopened as we approach the post-industrial age. The drive for equality of opportunity and modernisation has led to bigger schools. That trend is being reinforced by the need for economy in times of economic crisis, because larger schools are deemed to benefit from what economists call the economies of scale. It is also held that large schools can assemble more teaching facilities and offer a wider range of choices. In Britain, these trends have produced large, sometimes enormous, comprehensive schools (with up to two thousand pupils) as the norm of public secondary education. Against the gloomy background of unemployment, many of these huge establishments are lawless and loveless places, offering little contact between pupils and teachers, between the schools and their social environment and even among pupils themselves.

A wide range of solutions are on offer. Governments are trying to make schools more relevant and useful; in Britain a Conservative government has conducted a drive to teach children to be enterprising, especially in business. This effort has the support of some people in the wholistic movement, but it strikes others as inadequate as well as too firmly anchored in the capitalist ideology. At the radical extreme, Ivan Illich proposes to deschool society altogether, offering instead an a-la-carte system of self-education.

A more practical approach is taken by the movement for human-scale education. This movement, close to the mainstream of wholistic thinking, wants schools that will be not only small, but firmly anchored in their communities. These are to be schools on the wholistic model of society, which rejects the separation of the classroom from the world outside. The movement follows the ideas of Schumacher, who insisted that institutions should be appropriately sized for human usefulness. This movement also follows Schumacher in wanting to break out of the narrow, academic and materialistic framework of existing curricula.

Professor Charles Handy of the London Business School, whom we met in chapter four as a campaigner for new attitudes to work, is also concerned about the dismal aspect of contemporary British state education:

> To be a pupil in a large school is a strange experience. How many of us, if asked to organise an office, would so arange things that people worked for eight or nine bosses in a week, in perhaps five different work groups, in seven different rooms, without any desk or chair to call their own, no place for their belongings and discouraged if not prohibited, from talking to anyone while working? Furthermore, which of us, would then interrupt them thirty minutes into each task and move them onto the next? Only slightly caricatured, that is the experience of a pupil in a large secondary school...(1)

Handy concludes that the British system is out of date, with pernicious results.

> The British educational system today probably harms more people than it helps. That is not intentional. The teaching profession is, on the whole, both diligent and dedicated; it is the fault of the system, designed at other times for other purposes...In 1981, as proudly recorded in *Social Trends 1983*, 51% of boys and 56% of girls left school with at least one O' level or CSE Grade I. The other side of that coin is the shameful truth—49% of all boys and 44% of all girls left school as failures without a single worthwhile certificate to their names. The great bulk of them became the 40 % of our youth who receive no further training at all in life after the age of 14 - 40% of the nation written off educationally. (2)

EDUCATION FOR ENTERPRISE

One response by the British government has been to adapt the examination system to make it less academic. The new GCSE examination is indeed more flexible, and a more realistic guide to relevant ability than the old O' Levels.

Another approach has been to train pupils for the world of business while still at school. The aim was set out in a White Paper in 1985.

These efforts win the approval of Guy Dauncey, whom we have met as an organiser and propagandist of the self-help society. He was enthusiastic when he told us:

> The key idea is action learning. Experience learning. Key changes have been made in Scotland through Education Enterprise methods. They teach kids business in practice: they raise shares at 50p a share; decide what to make; or what service to offer. The kids have the right to do it, to make a profit or loss, with no judgement of what's right or what's wrong. They come to life: learning is real; it's their own project. They have a 'Minico Kit'—that stands for mini company or mini co-operative. There's one vote per share. The Manpower Services Commission also has its TVEI (Technical Vocational Educational Institute) & CPVE. They're for kids who won't be taking exams. It is the biggest revolution we've had for 600 years in education. It leads to a fuller education than the exam stuff. Otherwise, people are on the streets after O' and A' level. This offers team work, responsibility, thinking for themselves, a broader education. . . 50,000 kids went through CPVE.

The Young Enterprise scheme, based on a similar American idea known as 'Junior Achievement', was training more than seventeen thousand youngsters in 1985, involving more than seven hundred companies. The scheme encourages senior pupils to set up businesses with a small share capital, advises them, but leaves them in overall control for one academic year before the company is wound up. The companies are sponsored by established firms.

Enterprise education does not go far enough, according to some critics. The Social Democratic politician, Shirley Williams, has called for the MSC's training scemes to come under the direct control of the Education Ministry, "to heal the academic-vocational divide".*(The Times 25/3/86)* Other critics find these training schemes too crudely capitalist in inspiration. The National Union of Teachers objects:

> To see education as the instrument to fulfil the industrial and economic needs of the country is to regard individuals only in terms of these socio-economic roles and the education service as an agency to satisfy the government's manpower plans. . . The application of the principles of the White Paper would produce young people of conformist views trained in skills which might or might not be useful in the world of employment or unemployment in which they find themselves, but without the ability to participate in activities which would release their creative energies as individuals with unique contributions to make to their communities. (3)

The Union's misgivings are reflected in the disillusionment of many young people when they graduate from business training at school to the Youth Training Scheme, which often strikes them as a facade to hide unemployment. Chris and Jude, two young YTS trainees, told Margaret Thatcher how they felt in a poem:

> Look at all Maggie's done,
> I'd like to go out and buy a gun,
> Unemployment, drugs and drink,
> It's enough to make you stop and think.
>
> Walk about the streets at night,
> Probably end up in a fight.
> Nothing to do, nowhere to go,
> We all have the rights as well you know.
>
> All we got offered is YTS,
> It's enough to make you feel depressed.

No real jobs anywhere you go.
£27 - that's pretty low.

A tenner a week for your board,
You soon get pissed off and very bored.
Look at all the things it's meant to cover,
You end up getting a sub off your mother.

We're all heading on the same boat,
We should have the right just to vote.
It's the same old words and excuses,
We don't count, they just use us. (4)

The last line of the poem is bitter, expressing what so many young people are brought up to feel. This is more than an indictment of the class system of British education: it is despair over a whole society.

THE DESCHOOLERS

Radical reformers like Ivan Illich insist that a society has the schools it deserves; a consumer society educates its children to 'fit' into it, primarily as consumers. Illich condemns, "the hidden curriculum which serves as a ritual of initiation into a growth-orientated consumer society for rich and poor alike". He suggests that schools, because of their authoritarian structure, transform their originally humane purposes into repression. Teachers are forced to become custodians; the examination system does not evaluate ability or motivation so much as young peoples' capacity to fit into the social pyramid. People who have passed through the Western systems have learnt to label themselves clever or inferior. They have been taught to compete rather than co-operate. In addition, schools are a monopoly, preventing other channels from being used.

Classroom attendance removes children from the everyday world of Western culture and plunges them into an environment far more primitive, magical and deadly serious. School could not create such an enclave within which the rules of ordinary reality are suspended unless it physically incarcerated the young during many successive years on sacred territory. (5)

Illich wants education to work in the manner of webs instead of the manner of funnels. Instead of schools, he proposes 'skill exchanges' and 'learning webs' where students learn what they want to learn, actively, not passively, together with others who share their interests. He suggests that learning partners can be found by computer and selected tutors paid for by vouchers issued by the authorities. Some of Illich's proposals have been adopted in free schools in Europe and America and deschooling movements have been influential in China and India. But most of the proposals have proved impracticable in the long run, because they are not compatible with existing society. Few working parents could leave their children on their own. In an Illich structure, older children would, as often as not, succumb to the peer group mentality and would do nothing. Many adults, denied the use of an educational establishment, would be unable to use the stores of data-banked material. The deschoolers assume a degree of motivation that is not seen in present society, where public libraries are not flooded with eager deschoolers and museums find it difficult to attract clients.(An exception in Britain are the Adult Education Centres and the Workers Educational Association, which attract many people but are seriously underfunded.) The ideas of the deschoolers would work for a homogenous, human-scale society, with sure values and stable families; they cannot work in disparate urban communities. Illich's attack on the school system is in reality an attack on the whole of society, its utopian vision is of only limited value as a means of reforming our present system.

THE SCHUMACHER APPROACH

Fritz Shumacher had a different approach. His criticisms were not of the schools or the teachers, but of the content of education. He assumed that no amount of tinkering with schools could produce citizens fit for human-scale society, because they will have learned throughout their schooling the values which reinforce consumer society. Schumacher observed that the need for more and more scientists has blinded society to the fact that scientific know-how, valuable as it is, cannot transmit ideas of value, of knowing what to do with our lives.

> The way in which we experience and interpret the world obviously depends very much indeed on the kind of ideas that fill our minds. If they are mainly small, weak, superficial and incoherent, life will appear insipid, uninteresting, petty and chaotic. It is difficult to bear the resultant feeling of emptiness and the vacuum of our minds may only too easily be filled by some big fantastic notion—political or otherwise—which suddenly seems to illumine everything and to give meaning and purpose to our existence. It needs no emphasis that herein lies one of the great dangers of our time. (6)

Schumacher blames six leading ideas, developed in the nineteenth century, for the spiritual impasse in our education. They are all hypotheses and not open to proof; nevertheless they are generally accepted as though they were proven, with the result that whatever doctoring is done to the syllabus, whether the educators are politically right or left, whether the school is richly or poorly funded, a similar type of mind will be produced. These are the concepts:
1. The idea of evolution—that higher forms continually develop out of lower forms. This biological reference has come to be applied to every other aspect of reality.

2. The idea of natural selection and survival of the fittest, which is used to explain evolution and development.

3. Marx's political analysis, which reinterprets human history as the history of class struggles.

4. Freudian ideas which, reacting against the Marxist emphasis on economic struggle, reduce our efforts to the results of unfulfilled incest-wishes during childhood and early adolescence.

5. The idea that everything is relative and the consequent denial of absolutes, which tends to dissolve both norms and standards.

6. The idea of positivism, which assumes valid knowledge can be attained only through scientific methods and observable facts.

Schumacher does not deny the important elements of truth and usefulness in these key ideas of our civilisation. What he complains about is that "their essential character is their claim to universality". Their uncritical acceptance leads to a situation where "it is meaningless to say that man should aim at the 'higher' rather than the 'lower' because no intelligible meaning can be attached to purely subjective notions like higher or lower while the word 'should' is just a sign of authoritarian meglomania". (7) The result is a view of the world as a wasteland in which there is no meaning and purpose, in which man's consciousness is an unfortunate cosmic accident, in which despair and anguish are the only final realities. Schumacher insists that education should lead to spiritual awareness:

> The great ideas of the nineteenth century may fill our minds
> in one way or another, but our hearts do not believe in them
> all the same. Mind and heart are at war with one another,
> not, as is commonly asserted, reason and faith. Our reason
> has become clouded by an extraordinary, blind and
> unreasonable faith in a set of fantastic and life-destroying
> ideas inherited from the nineteenth century. It is the foremost

task of our reason to recover a truer faith than that. (8)

How can we discover which values to adopt? Schumacher draws a distinction between convergent and divergent problems and solutions. Convergent problems are those whose solution converge the more they are studied, such as Pythagoras' theorem, the formula for penicillin or the design of a space shuttle. Once the answers have been found they can be formulated and passed down on to others. Most scientific knowledge consists of convergent problem solving and most of what we overtly teach our children in schools is problem solving of that nature. Divergent problems cannot be solved by linear, rational thought. They deal with concepts like love, beauty, truth, honour and justice. Schumacher concludes: "The true problems of living—in politics, economics, education, marriage etc.—are always problems of overcoming or reconciling opposites. They are divergent problems and have no solution in the ordinary sense of the word." (9)

In trying to decide how to structure our educational system, we have a clear example of divergent problem solving. Schumacher suggests what might happen if we asked several highly intelligent and thoughtful people how to educate our children. Some may well reply that education is a process enabling our existing culture to be transmitted to the new generation. An equally well meaning and intelligent group of advisors will tell us that education is a facility. The young child, like the young plant, needs the best possible conditions and the utmost freedom in which to develop his or her innate capacities. The minimum interference and the maximum freedom will produce the best results. Schumacher points out that the former case, taken to its logical conclusion, would produce a prison and the latter a wilderness or a state of chaos.

In the schools and colleges of today, one can find both tendencies. Is there any prospect of reconciliation of these opposites: of freedom v. obedience; child-centred v. teacher-orientated; structure v. informality? Schumacher wanted us to revise our whole concept of education, but offered few practical suggestions. The gap remains, as Maurice Ash argues in a recent book: "no bridge of discourse has yet been found between an education with an ethic founded on the person and one founded on society". (10) People who are trying to build that bridge and to build a model of schooling that could fit into our present society, are organizing the movement for human-scale education.

THE HUMAN-SCALE MOVEMENT

A new movement for human-scale education is centred at Hartland, the North Devon village where Satish Kumar and other parents founded The Small School in 1982. The movement combines the aims of human-scale with those of Schumacher, Handy and others who want more relevant and wholistic curricula and schools more firmly anchored in communities. The importance of the Small School is that it shows such a model is workable in Britain today, even though such a school could flourish still better in a more humane society. The movement is in part a protest against official attitudes which apply the principle of cost-effectiveness in closing down village schools, arguing that the true criterion should be cost-benefit.

Originally a three-part alliance was formed between disciples of Schumacher campaigners for keeping small schools open and education officials, dissatisfied with excessive centralisation and creeping giantism. Philip Toogood is part of the movement. In 1982 he was forced out as headmaster of Madeley Court comprehensive school in Telford new town, Shropshire, after he had broken it down into autonomous learning units. The nucleus of the movement also includes John Watts, who did for

Countersthorpe School in Leicester what Toogood did for Madeley Court. The result, he claimed, was that a network of 'learning families' was substituted for the monolith; vandalism disappeared and exam results improved.

Human-scale education flourishes in community schools as well as small schools. A traditional strand of community-based education in Britain is inspired from Dartington, where Leonard Elmshirst liberally funded a home for artists and a progressive school. But this venture did not grow into a national movement. A second strand was the provision of community colleges, funded by the county councils. The prime mover here was the educational reformer Henry Morris, who, as far back as the 1920s, had wanted to stem the depopulation of rural England by the revitalisation of rural communities through village colleges. The first community college was opened at Sawston in 1930. The idea spread to towns like Coventry, Bristol and Manchester in the fifties and sixties, but the stringent economic conditions of the eighties have precluded widespread expansion. There are now about thirty community colleges in the United Kingdom. John Watts sees the requirements as far greater. "In the era of the micro chip, the challenge to community education may well be less that of providing variety in recreational activity than of how to equip the individual with the skills and insights that will enable him to choose when, how and where to work, whether remunerated or not." He also feels our consumer society has robbed people of the possibility of making their own amusement, (11)

The Small School at Hartland was founded to stop village children being bussed fifteen miles to the one thousand eight hundred-pupil comprehensive school at Bideford. Shareholders in the project raised the money to buy the building . The operating budget, much smaller than that of a state or normal private school, is met partly from private grants, partly from fees from those parents who can afford to pay. Some villagers send fresh vegetables for the school dinners, others teach at the school or invite pupils to learn at their homes or businesses. The children spend part of each day in outside lessons and practical activities.

The only compulsory subject for the twenty-six boys and girls are Maths, English and cooking. School dinners, including home-baked bread are prepared each day by one adult and two children. Colin Hodgetts, one of the two full-time teachers (there are seven part-time, in addition to local people who help out in their own fields) thinks cooking fulfils pupils' need to give as well as to receive. Cooking gets instant appreciation and is also a basic survival skill for the modern world. Children at the Small School can take national exams in subjects of their choice if and when they wish. For Colin Hodgetts, only human-scale education on this pattern allows a teacher to do his or her real job.

> The nature of the relationship between teacher and pupil is determined primarily by the teacher. To be relaxed and open means for the teacher, to be vulnerable. With teachers, as with social workers, there is a temptation to hide behind a professional mask. A primary head told me recently that she had given up living in the same village as her school as it was like being in a goldfish bowl. Only one other head present in the group at the conference we were attending lived where he worked. This is one small example of the distancing that teachers find it necessary to establish between themselves and their charges...It is teaching itself that reveals to us our own inadequacies and our powerlessness. It is from a base of powerlessness that we, without seeking to be, are of help. The teacher must become human, giving up aspirations to infallibility. (12)

In a Manifesto in 1986, the movement for human-scale education deplored the tendency towards small school closures. The authors supported the egalitarian principle behind comprehensive schools, but complained that efforts to include the widest possible variety of subjects had led to schools that were over-sized and unmanageable. The effects have been felt in bureaucratisation, ill-disipline and strained relations between teachers and children, between teachers and parents and between the school and the community. The negative influence of large-scale schooling was also visible in truancy, vandalism and violence. Many pupils were dismissing school as an inflexible institution where they matter little and learn less, becoming altogether alienated from the values enshrined in the school. The manifesto set out seven benefits of human-scale schooling:

1. Personal contact with individual children becomes unavoidable and good relationships are more easily established. Education and welfare can be more naturally integrated with the same adults teaching the children and caring for their general well-being.

2. A more active style of learning, increased group and independent learning can be encouraged without elaborate structures of control.

3. Without the rigidities of an elaborate timetable, individuality in the context of learning and rhythm of learning can be extended.

4. Education for social responsibility can start from a young age because pupils can be given a say in decisions affecting them or the whole school without resorting to cumbersome consultation procedures.

5. Small schools need to use parents and other adults in the community to supplement the teachers work and to use community facilities to supplement their own. The consequence is a greater involvement of the children in the community and a more natural 'real life' curriculum for them.

6. Parents have a real choice when there are several smaller schools.

7. A good standard of discipline is easier to establish and maintain. Because of increased contact and better

relationships between adults and children, teachers have an improved opportunity to encourage good behavior. Conversely, children will be less inclined to misbehave in order to be noticed.

These benefits offset many criticisms of small schools that they can be too narrow in the scope of subjects offered and that small numbers of pupils can create stifling peer groups.

HUMAN SCALE IN PRACTICE

Human-scale education, like all the other strands in wholistic thinking, stands mid-way between theory and practice. The idea of human-scale schools is not new, nor is it absent from many existing state-sector as well as private schools. In some schools, teachers do what they can in unpromising surroundings; in others, bold experiments have been toned down and muted in practice. Experimental schools nearly always attract the rejects of the prevailing system, giving their work an uphill direction.

The White Lion Free School of Islington, London, reflects many of these problems. This school, in a depressed inner-city area, is barely supported by the borough council, which will only accord it the status of a youth centre. The school is run on completely non-authoritarian lines, but this poses problems for many of the older children, who are self-rejects from the state system.

The free school started in the early seventies in the wave of optimism that still carried over from the sixties. The idea was: "we must get away from factory models of education, from generalised pre-packed curricula, from petty rules, corporal punishment, rigid hierarchical structures". (13)

There is no head teacher. Major decisions are taken at weekly meetings by a consensus. In line with the founding ideas, no one opinion carries more weight than another. The eight full-time staff call themselves 'workers,' not teachers, because they perform tasks like cooking, clerical work, caretaking and maintenance. They accept very low salaries.

The school was founded as a community school, with parents free to come in when they like, participate, share skills or learn with the children. The workers wanted the school to stay open most of the time, evenings and weekends. However, after a year they found many of these ideas did not work. There was not enough community response. Workers found they became burnt out and several had to leave because of the strain.

Mornings are for lessons, in which learning centres round four subjects: 'the body', 'jobs', 'thinking' and 'the future'. Afternoons are spent in activies like music, and pottery and outings including zoos, cinemas, theatres, a city farm and Hampstead Heath.

The thirty children, aged from three to sixteen, are supposed to come from a one thousand yard radius around the school, but the rule is flexible and numbers are increasing to fifty. Many of the nursery-age children have parents who believe in the school's ideals, but further up the age range there are children who have refused to stay at state schools and these can be difficult to reach.

The Free School has always been short of money. The building itself is a fine, two hundred-year-old listed town house on three floors, but the children have no playground. The interior, although brightly painted, is cramped, the walls scratched and the skirtings scuffed. The structure of the building militates against the way the workers want to run the school. There are no posters brightening up the walls, "the children tear them down", we were told. The midday meal is taken on the ground floor in a room which serves for meetings and canteen. The noise is deafening. A worker said: "there's a lot of confusion about acting out agression and bad feelings. The freedom here requires a great deal of self-awareness and self-esteem. If the kids haven't got that—it's very hard for them."

Ordinary state schools can be wholistic, even if they sometimes have to compromise with the prevailing culture. We found that at Fiveways Primary School on the outskirts of Colchester, in Essex, in a mixed area of new housing estates, rural villas and Edwardian villas. Peter Anderson, the headmaster, had not heard of *Small is Beautiful* when we visited Fiveways, yet he attempts a a human-scale school, "I see it as a community school. It's a coming together place, with no separation between home, school and community." He encourages parents' participation in the running of the school. On the day we visited, the children were preparing a harvest tea for their grandparents. The hall was decorated, cakes were being baked and the choir was practising.

> The parents recently raised £1000 for an adventure playground. It's not just that they collect money for the big things: they help all the time. Of course the parents round here are upwardly mobile. The parents at some of my former schools thought of school as a place of failure. Here they will accept new ideas, but you have to go slowly. My teachers call me 'Peter' but on the PTA it has to be Mister Anderson, otherwise other parents might get jealous. When you are working in the mainstream whatever ideas you have—you've got to bring the others in slowly.

A feature of this school is the extreme care with which the objects and artifacts are looked after and displayed. Peter wants the environment to reflect order, comfort and beauty. He works towards an attitude of freedom for rather than freedom from. 'Child-centred' schooling is not a new idea. It is practiced at Summerhill and many schools. Generally, progressive education has been the prerogative of the middle and upper classes. Peter Anderson is bringing ideas of community and parent involvement into a State Primary and he is succeeding. He was born near Colchester and married another teacher, whom he had met at College. Until their youngest child starts schools, Peter's wife is staying at home, growing vegetables and milking the goats. He says she's happy. He is. "I'm working where I grew up."

SMALL SCHOOLS IN DENMARK

Small schools are a matter of course in Denmark, where they have grown out of a national awareness. More than eight per cent of the country's children and over twenty per cent of children in Copenhagen attend private schools in which the parents are bound to come together to thrash out policy. The cost of sending a child to a Danish independent school costs a parent something like £30 a month. Normally, the second child sent from a family attracts a big discount, and so on, until the fourth will go quite free. The state funds these schools to the tune of about eighty per cent of their expenditure. Richard North has written on these Danish schools:

> The heart of what I want to say about the Danish experience is that the business of coming together to fund and run small schools, the necessary compromises involved, the essential co-operativeness required, the rather high-minded pragmatism it betokens, are all exactly the sort of enterprise that the British—I mean, me and my neighbours and for all I know, you and yours—probably both badly need and could hugely enjoy...Independent small schools are as—perhaps more—necessary in Hackney as in Hampstead, in Kennington as in Kensington. The act of building such a school would demonstrate that English men and women, whether their grandparents were born in Bombay, Brixton, Barbados or Berkshire, could build a community around the shared enterprise of providing for their children's education. (14)

Which comes first? Can education transform society, or must we first wait for a new society? It is an old riddle. Today, the ideas and experience of the movement for 'education on a human scale' strongly suggest that both must change simultaneously. That will be the challenge of the 21st century.

Notes:

(1) Handy, *The Future of Work*.
(2) ibid.,
(3) *Better Schools, An Alternative View* NUT.
(4) *Scan*, May, 1985, No.159.
(5) Illich, *Deschooling Society*, page 19.
(6) Schumacher, *Small is Beautiful*, page 68.
(7) ibid, page 73.
(8) ibid, page 76.
(9) Schumacher, *Guide for the Perplexed*, page 81.
(10) Ash, *The New Renaissance*, page 178.
(11) Simon, *Education in the Eighties*.
(12) *Resurgence*, Aug/Sep 1986.
(13) *White Lion Free school Bulletin*. No. 2, page 6.
(14) *Resurgence*, Aug/Sep 1986.

CHAPTER THIRTEEN

The Spiritual Dimension

Path Through the Esk Valley

The Spiritual Dimension

HUMAN-SCALE thinking must have spiritual content. If we are to move from partial, fragmented, compartmentalised living towards completeness and wholistic living, we have to put back what our dominant industrial-materialist-scientific world-view leaves out. That world-view is not wrong, any more than science is wrong or capitalism or socialism are wrong; its shortcoming is in what it omits. That omitted area is what we mean by spiritual.

In that sense, the spiritual is not identified with any actual religion, nor confined to religious sentiment; it includes the intuitive, the non-measurable, the aesthetic, the caring and the loving. All these aspects of our consciousness have been progressively relegated in our world to the domain of the private, subjective, even secret world of the individual. They are not considered to have direct relevance to society, except in churches. They have been demoted to the second class of values, after demand and supply, freedom and mobility, comfort and welfare, education and health.

The loss is immense, almost impossible to comprehend or define. Erich Fromm, as we saw in chapter two, attempts an understanding in terms of our passage from the concept of *being*, which embraces the whole of us, to one of *having*, which is only a part. Instead of being healthy we think of ourselves as having health. Instead of knowing, we are taught we have knowledge. When he tries to pinpoint that unhappy transition, Fromm discovers that the Hebrews have no word for having; for 'I have,' they can only say yeish-li, 'there is to me.' As Schumacher also noted, the Israelites invented the notion of 'to each according to his needs', later rediscovered by the Marxists.

The spiritual loss involved in industrialisation has been lamented by many writers, notably R.H.Tawney in *Religion and the Rise of Capitalism.* They lament the transition when, as Fromm put it, "reason began to deteriorate into manipulative intelligence and individualism into selfishness". Our Protestant work ethic culminated in giving people what Fromm called a 'marketing character', experiencing oneself as a commodity and one's value not as use-value but as exchange-value. Fromm is here in the heart of Schumacher territory.

The arch-rebel against industrial degradation in the last century was Marx. But Fromm saw Marx and Engels as coming a century too soon; for their ideas, embedded in the nineteenth century, could not avoid taking on the 'capitalist spirit' and socialism has indeed been tinged with the capitalist spirit ever since: both systems are rooted in the *having* mode and in economic growth. The radical humanists later widened the scope of the protest against the industrial ethos. Albert Schweitzer re-launched the human-scale revolution by insisting that production ought to serve peoples' real needs; that there must be a new relationship with nature; that solidarity must replace antagonism; and that there must be sane consumption and active individual participation in society. (1)

Today, as we have argued in this book, capitalism is well past its prime, creating the possibility of a more radical change of mind-set. The need to rediscover a proper social role for the spiritual is not just a matter of peoples' private wellbeing; it is a matter of survival in a nuclear age. A spiritual dimension is as necessary in socialist countries as in capitalist ones and here Rudolf Bahro is a witness. Bahro came to share William Reich's view of the character structure and knowledge structure of our societies as competitive and conflict-oriented, and of our economic expansion as a 'fleeing forwards'. Bahro sees exemplary figures in any society, including Christ and Buddha, as seeking the new man "not by looking forwards, but by looking backwards or inwards—in other words, they divested themselves of the conditions which society imposed on them from birth".

> We have to find a way for all humans to make the
> breakthrough that Christ and Buddha did. The existence of
> Christ, or Buddha or St Francis of Assisi, demonstrates that
> it is possible for humans to deal with the aggressive warlike
> quality they have as humans. Must it always be minorities
> that achieve this? Or it it possible for us to organise
> consciously towards this end? Without conscious organisation,
> without institutionalisation, it is not possible to achieve this. (2)

Here is the meeting point between spiritual needs and social organisation. Institutions, not just individuals, have to be organised in harmony with spiritual as well as material needs. Echoing Schumacher, Bahro continues:

> The problem is not the abolition of technology but its
> subordination. Our aim has to be 'the reconstruction of
> God'—in other words, the kind of regulation which can only
> come from the re-creation of spiritual equilibrium, within
> those levels of nature neglected by Marx where human
> consciousness comes into contact with the external world. (3)

Another requirement for human survival, as our own book has shown, is a deeper awareness of the natural environment. And here, too, there can be no awareness which is not spiritual; otherwise we are talking yet again, of a quantifiable commodity called environment and of a department of life instead of life itself. The American ecological writers make this point with the greatest eloquence. Robinson Jeffers wrote:

> I believe that the Universe is one being, all its parts are
> different expressions of the same energy, and they are all in
> communication with each other, therefore parts of one organic
> whole. (This is physics, I believe, as well as religion.)...This
> whole is in all its parts so beautiful, and if felt by me to be so
> intensely in earnest, that I am compelled to love it, and to
> think of it as divine. It seems to me that this whole alone is
> worthy of the deeper sort of love; and that there is peace,
> freedom, I might say a kind of salvation, in turning one's
> affections outward towards this one God, rather than inwards
> on one's self, or on humanity, or on human imaginations and
> abstractions—the world of spirits. I think that it is our
> privilege and felicity to love God for his beauty, without
> claiming or expecting love from him. We are not important to
> him, but he to us. I think that one may contribute (ever so
> slightly) to the beauty of things by making one's own life and
> environment beautiful, so far as one's power reaches. (4)

We are talking about attention to spiritual needs which is ecologically aware, but not necessarily linked to an established religion. Those who agree do not normally start from revelation or from mystic experience; they start from the material world of people, animals, plants and landscape. They find, as Schumacher did on a visit to Leningrad, that our official map of reality is woefully incomplete. Everywhere in Leningrad, Schumacher saw churches; but these large landmarks, so obvious to his eye, had not been included on his Intourist map. He was reminded of the missing landmarks on the official maps of our civilisation. Everything which is subjective, which cannot not be proved, is left out.

A Guide for the Perplexed was Schumacher's last book, published posthumously. Decades earlier, his thinking had started in the very material world of economics, when he was economic advisor to the National Coal Board. He had begun with the absurdities of social and economic organisation: the waste of resources, the inhuman scale of economic organisation, the dehumanising effects of industrial work. Later, after visits to India and other parts of Asia, he began to think in a world context. But all the time he was delving deeper, towards the essence: the staggering incompleteness of our society's vision of human nature: we were navigating with maps that left out out the crucial landmarks. (5)

In *Good Work* he reached the conclusion that "the most urgent need of our time is and remains the need for metaphysical reconstruction—a supreme effort to bring clarity into our deepest convictions with regard to the questions, What is man? Where does he come from? And what is the purpose of his life?" Our education, he lamented, was dismissing "as pre-scientific and therefore not to be taken seriously" what was in fact the kernel of human wisdom, an innate knowledge of the divine that had matured over millenia. And so, in his last book, Schumacher sets out to draw a proper map.

As his base line he takes the ancient hierarchy of being: mineral, plant, animal, and human. At the pinnacle of earthly life, he places human consciousness and self-awareness and he situates faith, as St Augustine did, at the heart of understanding.

From this point Schumacher builds another hierarchy: the levels of knowing. First, you must know yourself, a knowledge which requires an adequate 'organ of cognition' if it is not to fall into the shortcomings of modern science and leave out the essentials. Knowing yourself in this full sense is the first field of knowldege. Having understood yourself, you can go on to the next field: understanding the 'invisible person who is your neighbour'. But the first field and therefore also the second, are subjective, so we require a third field in which we know ourselves as we are known by others. For this we need to go beyond consciousness to self-awareness, without which we could be prey to 'the grossest and most destructive illusions'. With this third field, Schumacher tries to avoid the pitfalls of mysticism. He leaves to the last the field of observable, exterior reality which is the preserve of science. (6)

Since Schumacher, all major writers on new economics, human-scale education, grassroots development, complementary medicine and related topics have acknowledged that their subject has a spiritual content. Does this trend reflect a more general spiritual awakening? Is there a New Age, to use an expression common in green-thinking ventures? Is there really an 'Aquarian conspiracy,' as described by the elegiac American writer, Marilyn Ferguson? Is there a turning point, as advocated by Fritjof Capra? Is there, as all these and many other post-modern, post-industrialist writers assume, a new paradigm?

It is healthy to be sceptical about paradigms, because the word has been overworked since Thomas Kuhn introduced it in 1970 to define a scientific consensus that determines, crucially, what questions scientists ask. (7)

Kuhn's concept has since been abusively enlarged to embrace the subjective label anyone can stick on the infinite complexity of what people actually think. A change of world view, the substitution of a new set of values, a new mindset, cannot readily be identified while the process is happening. It is all too easy to see one's own paradigm everywhere. The major paradigm changes so far identified in our civilisation have been the transition from the ancient world to the Judaeo-Christian and that from the Judeao-Christian to the scientific post-Enlightenment age. At first sight it seems hazardous to assume anything so momentous today. The flowering of alternative thinking, which began in much of the world in the 1960's, is not immediately apparent in the

1980's; the flower people have wilted, the hippy communes have been disbanded and the turbulent students have returned to their classes. With the onset of economic recession, electorates have become more cautious and conservative.

Yet it would be equally short-sighted to assume that the ferment is over. Many of the hard-core rebels of the 1960's are still active in more mature ways. Some have moved out of the rat race and away from media attention, to the country. Some are members of more mature communities, as we saw in chapter four.

But what of ordinary people. who still lead conventional lives? Do they really accept the materialist-industrialist world view? Or do they only pretend, because there is no socially acceptable way of differing? Opinion polls in Europe and the USA consistently show that most people believe in God, though most do not attend church regularly, if at all. How do they worship their God? Nobody knows, because this is the private, subjective realm that society leaves alone. Religious cults and house churches have drawn in those who find established religion too remote, too rigid in its theology and ritual too irrelevant. Many people are finding a compromise between unthinking materialism and unthinking religion, difficult to achieve.

Recent discussion of these issues in *The Guardian's* 'Face to Faith' column yielded a surprising number of letters from people,who said they were looking for a spiritual lead they could not find in the churches. It seems reasonable to assume that if people have begun to question the dominant world-view, but have no other in sight, they will suffer spiritual deprivation. William James pointed out at the beginning of this century that intuitive beliefs are more real to people than the officially acceptable 'truths' they may espouse in public. (8) Many writers since then have discussed the painful schizophrenia this situation has produced. Is this a cause of the prevailing despair?

The theologian Lesslie Newbigin said of his return to Britain after nearly forty years in India, that the first thing to strike him was the absence of hope. Analysing the causes of this hopelessness, Newbigin finds the essential change the Enlightenment introduced was the abandonment of the notion that everyone and everything are defined by their purpose. (9)

His point may sound abstruse. But it is surely not lost on people standing in a Liverpool dole queue. What, indeed, are they for? Newbigin says our culture has invented individual rights with no corresponding idea of who or what is to ensure them. All we have is the State, which "replaces the holy church and the holy empire... and since the pursuit of happiness is endless, the demands on the State are without limit... It has taken the place of God as the source to which we look for happiness, health and welfare". (10)

Today the inadequacy of the State is all too evident. Opinion polls constantly confirm that people, on the political Left as well as Right, are losing confidence in institutions, like political parties, social services and churches.

Nobody has yet disproved the dominant scientific-materialist world-view of the industrial age; but there are signs that it has been discredited and destabilised. Numerous commentators, erudite in both science and religion, have pointed out that this world view has failed to live up to its promises and by accepting its values unquestioningly, we have brought the world into an unprecedented mess. They argue, further, that modern science itself has reached frontiers where the distinction between the material and the non-material worlds is in doubt.

It does not follow that people should be flocking back into the churches. These appear firmly stuck in the musty idiom of a pre-scientific world that can never return. Yet at least one explorer of the new convergence of science and religion, Keith Ward, Professor of History and Philosophy of Religion at King's College London, finds that the 'reinvigoration' of faith in contemporary Britain is nothing short of a revolution, even if it is more evident in senior common rooms than in the size of congregations. "Our faith in science remains intact," Ward concludes, "but our faith in the values which gave birth to science, in our ability to control the progress of science, in human reason itself, has been undermined." (11)

Ward finds that the relentless progress of reason over the centuries has itself served to undermine reason. This seeming paradox began happening as a result of Darwin's view of evolution, with the message that human progress has depended largely on chance. It was carried further by modern psychology and biology, with their suggestion that the irrational and the purely chemical in us reign supreme.

You do not have to be a professor to see where the materialist, science-based world view has got us. There are plenty of negative arguments against the prevailing paradigm. The positive argument is that science itself, notably in quantum physics and relativity, has reached the frontiers of materialism. After Einstein, nothing is as solid as it seems: matter is energy and energy is matter. The classic quantum experiment shows sub-atomic particles behaving as matter when observed in one way and as waves when observed in another. The observer affects what she observes. The particles conform to wave patterns with no physically discernable instruction to do so, as if they 'knew', as if something non-material was active. Ward quotes Paul Davies, Professor of Theoretical Physics at Newcastle Upon Tyne, as admitting to him that such happenings in the sub-atomic world cannot be explained by chance. "Something is going on," Davies told Ward: "As far as physics is concerned, mechanistic materialism has been dead for 50 years...the old-fashioned paradigm of a clockwork universe slavishly unfolding according to the laws of cause and effect has been demolished".

Davies has explained elsewhere about quantum theory:

Its fascination is that it seems to undermine the basis of commonsense reality. Quantum physics reveals that on an atomic scale the apparently concrete world of daily experience dissolves away into ghostly patterns of vibrating energy. Concepts such as motion or location in space become fuzzy and ill-defined. More significantly, the theory makes no clear distinction between the whole and its parts, or between observer and observed. Quantum physics seems to weave the entire cosmos into an indivisible unity. (12)

The new framework supports the view that physical reality is not, after all, made of building blocks of matter whose behaviour can be observed objectively, explained and predicted. This discovery undermines the reductionist approach that has guided science since the Enlightenment, the assumption that nature can best be understood by reducing matter to its smallest components and observing these objectively. It now appears that the smallest sub-atomic particles cannot be observed without being affected by the observer. Nor does a particle of matter really exist outside its function in a universe that appears increasingly organic. That brings physics back face to face with metaphysics where it began and reintroduces God into the argument.

This convergance of science and religion imposes a challenge to both. The theologian Lesslie Newbigin argues in his book, *Foolishness to the Greeks,* that the scientific frontier "challenges theology in a new way to come out of its private enclave and say what it has to say about the world, about the single, finite entity the physicists call space-time, within which it is impossible to isolate a 'spiritual' from a 'material' world of space". Professor Ward, standing between the two cultures, calls for an end to the 'phantom battle' between them. On one side are scientists who continue to peer at tiny parts in isolation from the whole, ignoring purpose and origin. On the other are believers who still pretend evolution did not happen. The phantom battle, says Ward, is "between a very old-fashioned and imperialistic view of science and an equally old-fashioned and imperialistic view of religion".

The new science does not, of course, prove God; it merely restores importance and relevance to those human faculties that conceive God. Most importantly, the new science is turning its back on reductionism in favour of wholism. The traveller who has gone furthest along this road is David Bohm, Professor of Theoretical Physics at Birkbeck College, London. In *Wholeness and the Implicate Order*, Bohm takes issue with the 'commonsense' view that fragmentation is the reality while wholeness is an ideal to which we might strive. "What should be said is that wholeness is what is real, and that fragementation is the response of this whole to man's action, guided by illusory perception, which is shaped by fragmentary thought." Bohm concludes: "it is not an accident that our fragmentary form of thought is leading to such a widespread range of crises—social, political economic, ecological, psychological, etc...Such a mode of thought implies unending development of chaotic and meaningless conflict, in which the energies of all tend to be lost by movements that are antagonistic or else at cross purposes."

Do we need a new religion for the post-industrial age? There are indeed many signs of restiveness within established religions, and some of these imply dissatisfaction with an image of God that has become unacceptable in a scientific context. Theologians and scientists have tried to re-define God in such such phrases as 'the source of your ultimate concern, what you take seriously without reservation'. Einstein suggested: 'the central order of things and events'.

Many green-thinking people who identify themselves with a new age spirituality, notably in the influential Findhorn Foundation in northern Scotland, practise a personal faith that is rooted in nature and has echoes of vitalism and even pantheism. Findhorn began semi-miraculously in 1962 by 'communion with nature' that produced forty-pound cabbages and eight inch delphiniums in almost barren soil. Caroline Hall, a member, sums up her faith by analogy with a hologram, an idea widely used in wholistic thought. A hologram is a representation in which every detail contains a picture of the whole, unlike a photograph which produces an effect through individual dots, meaningless in isolation.

> Every part of our universe is a hologram. Each cell, each plant, each person contains a picture of the whole. So every time I experience God a little more, the universe experiences God a little more; each time I dissolve a negative thought form and replace it with knowledge of abundance, so I bring a bit more awareness of abundance into the planet. This is the central message of the Findhorn Foundation: you and I as individuals are vitally important to the growth and development of our world. The way I live my life, both inner and outer, can bring the world closer to God, or move us further away. (13)

Others in this movement have been influenced by the human potential movement of the sixties, which brought to the West many Eastern forms of thought, meditation and self-improvement. They are affected also by the new wholistic climate in the physical sciences and the prevailing mood of awareness of nature. This is the kind of faith held by Guy Dauncey. He told us:

> ...Underlying all my approach to economic development and community change is a very strong spiritual perception. For me there is no such thing as an atom that is only material. There has to be consciousness inside everything: evolution is co-evolution of matter and spirit. Before the Rennaissance the assumption was that the earth could not be transformed: you could only hope to leave it and go to heaven. Then came Bacon and the scientists and a deal was struck on the lines of the Cartesian division: we concern ourselves with things that

we can measure: you look after the spirit. Once the scientists broke away and were free to test things, they came up with their own miracles. Now we have fulfilled that stage and from 1963 onwards, from Rachel Carson's *Silent Spring*, from which I date the beginning of the environmental movement, people say: we've done that and now it's having negative effects. Many parts of the world still need to transform material reality, but we here have gone too far and we have to look at consequences. The quest now is for the soul to produce a better reality. We've done it on the material path; now the interest is in the invisible path. Hence the uprising of interest in the early sixties in non-tangible realities.

If a new, post-industrial religion is to emerge, it will have to be ecologically aware and in our shrunken world, it will have to be universalist. Many Christians are indeed becoming aware of the implications for ecology of the biblical injunction to dominate the earth, which is embedded deeply in our our Judeo-Christian religion. "Just as I gave you the green plants, I now give you everything," says the God of *Genesis* and the scientists took over from there. In 1986, the Church of England's General Synod showed it was worried about what is still called environmental issues (a safe phrase for tucking them away which even serious newspapers like *The Guardian* use). It approved a report, *Our Responsibility for the Living Environment*, which argued mildly that stewardship of Creation figures as prominently in the Bible as dominating the earth and was now more urgent.

Catholic writers are making the same point. That religion needs to speak of ecology, urgently while there is still time, is the passionate plea of Sean McDonagh, an Irish missionary working at the sharp end of third world anti-development projects in the Philippines. In *To Care for the Earth*, McDonagh argues that Christian theology went off the rails in its preoccupation with man's fall and redemption while almost forgetting creation, which means nature. "The

20 billion years of God's creative love is either seen simply as the stage on which the drama of human salvation is worked out, or as something radically sinful in itself and needing transformation." McDonagh wants an ecological revolution in church litany and the establishment of a feast of creation.

Many people who seek to modernise religion are influenced by ideas on the potential of human consciouness, developed by Teilhard de Chardin and popularised recently by Peter Russell in *The Awakening Earth*. Russell links these ideas with James Lovelock's hypothesis that the earth, or *Gaia*, behaves as a form of super-organism (see chapter six). Russell postulates, with more poetry than science, that if the world population stabilises at around ten billion by the late 21st century, it will have reached a figure that biology has shown in the past to be conducive to evolutionary leaps. So Gaia will make another such leap. "The human race may be fast approaching the stage where there are sufficient numbers of self-reflexive consciousnesses on the planet for the next level to emerge."

Russell argues that "as worldwide communication capabilities become increasingly complex, society is beginning to look more and more like a planetary nervous system. The global brain is being activated". Finally he looks forward to "the emergence of something way beyond even a single planetary consciounesss or Supermind—a completely new level of evolution, as different from consciousness as consciousness is from life, and life from matter". (14)

This is heady stuff, but open to cricisism because it presents an inspirational and optimistic view which could give the impression that mankind has nothing to worry about. There is another negative aspect of this human consciousness movement; it offers encouragement to the man-centred ethic of Judeo-Christianity, in which man has the right to dominate the rest of creation, animate and inanimate. Surely this is contrary to the spirit of *Gaia* as conceived by Lovelock. The ecological view is that people are part of nature; man is neither its creator nor its ruler. Because of this and other contradictions, we are still some way from the scientifically and ecologically aware religion many of us are searching for. But some major obstacles have been overcome. First, there is awareness of the need. Secondly, the world has shrunk to a size where no religion can prevail that is not of universal application. Thirdly, and most important, the concept of mind as distinct from brain, and therefore of intuition as distinct from reason and science, has been revived.

Notes:
(1) Fromm. *To Have or to Be*, page 15.
(2) Bahro *From Red to Green*, page 221.
(3) ibid, page 213.
(4) Sessions, *Deep Ecology*, page 101.
(5) Schumacher. *Guide For the Perplexed*, page 9.
(6) ibid, chapters 6-9.
(7) Kuhn, Thomas, *The Structure of Scientific Revolutions*, (University of Chicago Press, 1971).
(8) William James, *The Varieties of Religious Experience*, (Fount, 1901).
(9) Newbigin, *The Turn of the Tide*.
(10) Newbigin, *New Foolishness to the Greeks*, SPCK, 1986.
(11) Ward, *Turn of the Tide* .
(12) *The Guardian*, March 1987.
(13) *One Earth*, Findhorn Foundation Magazine, March/April 1986.
(14) Russell, *The Awakening Earth*.

CHAPTER FOURTEEN

Green Future

Derbyshire: Edale Valley, Denis Thorpe, The Guardian

Green Future

How do we start? By what imaginable transition can we move from here to a green future? Can the immense gap at least be narrowed, between the green-thinking dreamers and the present reality?

First, we need to agree that a green, or at least a greener future is desirable. The prospect has been attacked as boring, elitist, authoritarian, fascist, middle-class and even anti-feminist. Richard North, reacting against too much greenery in *The Guardian's Society Tomorrow* feature, *(12/10/85)* concludes that we are better off as we are:

A world in which co-operation is stressed over competition may well be so boring that it leads droves of men and women into risk-taking for the sheer fun of it; art and adventure, drugs and adultery have always been signs that men and women are bad at the business of living too reasonably. . . The problem is partly that we have under-appreciated the industrial world for its pleasures, opportunities and successes—while we have of course been assiduous, sometimes accurate, and often way off-beam in criticising it. Worse, I begin to think that we have been foolish enough to under-state the sheer value that attaches to us as members of the most splendid, beautiful hand elegant species that ever walked the earth. Dolphins are all very well, but build no cathedrals.

It is true that at present, most people in industrial countries have jobs and most of those with jobs manage to live a little better each year. Most of those who don't have jobs or decent incomes dream of joining those who do. And that optimistic objection to green ideas is balanced by a pessimistic one: that even people who might want to adopt a more wholistic and sustainable lifestyle cannot do so. They are stuck in cities. If they want to start a community business, they lack money and skills; if they want to grow food, they lack a garden; if they want to go and live in the country, they won't find a home they can afford and if they think of building one for themselves, they won't get planning permission.

The green vision can appear threatening. Trades unionists are naturally suspicious, in case it brings back a return to exploited, unorganised labour. Indeed the danger that some of the activities promoted in green thinking—home working, piece goods making, and part-time working—could degenerate into exploitation, is not lost on Greens themselves. They know that industrial countries could easily become two nations—the rich in the traditional economy, including its better and better paid workers and the alternatives. Ivan Illich warned that "indiscriminate propagation of self-help" would be "morally unacceptable" because it could create new drudgery, especially for women. It could become "the opposite of autonomous or vernacular self-help"(1)

'Neither left nor right, but forwards,' is the slogan British Greens have adopted from West German ones, and there is menace in that, too. The Left is suspicious of the reactionary streak which, as we have seen in our survey of ecologists, is latent in some green thinking. The Right is also wary, especially in West Germany, where Greens have a far

Left as well as a deeply conservative wing.

Some left-wing critics see the Greens as elitist, middle-class dreamers, concerned in their hearts to keep their country cottages safe from development. When we consulted Jonathon Porritt, the most down-to-earth of British Greens, he told us he is aware of the truth in that charge:

> I've been very critical of what I call the neo-Cotswolders, people who spend a large part of their life seeking arcadian retreats in the country and then spending the rest of their lives making damn certain that no-one else gets a share of it. I'm also very critical of the 'hands-off' ecological brigade who say that rural areas must remain pristine and untouched with no possibility for new light industry, new workshops...if we are going to bring about any kind of balance between rural and urban, if we are going to regenerate rural communities then we will only do that by providing access to good work.

Green thinking stands mid-way between the Marxist approach, change through society, and the religious approach, change through the individual. So it earns friends and enemies in both camps.

All these objections miss the crucial point: the have-nots in our society are not only the poor; they are the unhappy, the lonely, the frustrated, the alienated, the unfulfilled. They are the old people who fill our hospital wards, who wait in the doctor's waiting room with nothing wrong with them that a little love, or at least company would not cure. And if people yearn for change and see no way out, they can be shown how, as we have seen in our chapters on new ways of working and living in towns and countryside.

The green idea has made dramatic progress in politics throughout the world and Green politicians are now complaining of plagiarism. "There is a new consensus among all the big political parties that green is beautiful", said a Green Party pamphlet in 1986, while Ms. Jo Robins, a co-chairperson of the Party, complained in a press statement that everything in the Labour Party's 1986 policy statement on the environment, except a proposal for greater public involvement in planning, had been in the Greens' 1983 manifesto.

For his part, Jonathon Porritt refuses to complain about this plagiarism:

> I think there is a profound change going on in the Labour Party. Its latest document on the environment is an astonishing product and if even 50% of it was adopted as election manifesto it will mean profound changes for their attitudes towards industry, the economy, international affairs and so on. It's wrong to pretend that quite significant change is not happening, at that light-green, rather superficial level. What I think the Greens are in danger of doing is being very contemptuous of ways of bringing people through to ever deeper levels of awareness. You've got to provide doors for people, entranceways, to come into what amounts to a revolution in their thinking and attitudes. You can't just slap down this green thing as something totally different from what we're doing, that you have to embrace the whole or not all.

The Conservatives' 1987 election manifesto promised the following: continue modifying power stations to combat acid rain; improve standards for reducing pollution from cars; legislate on air pollution; double funding for environmentally sensitive areas; provide extra legal protection for National Parks; encourage small woodlands through grants; safeguard common land; support international action to protect atmosphere and seas; establish a National Rivers Authority and privatise water supply and sewage services; set up safe facilities for disposing of radioactive waste.

The Labour manifesto promised: to set up an Environmental Protection Service and a Wildlife and

Countryside Service; extend the planning system to cover agricultural forestry and water developments; invest more in land reclamation, recycling and conservation; act against acid rain; stop radioactive discharges as sea; improve monitoring and enforcement of pollution control; bring in a Wildlife and Countryside Act to give public access to all common land, mountain, moor and health; end all organised hunting with hounds; update animal protection laws.

The Green Party's much more radical 1987 manifesto proposed a Basic Income scheme and a Community Ground Rent designed to tax the added value of land. Income tax would be local, used for local purposes, and people could no longer make money simply by holding onto land.

All this political greenery could be explained as just a fashion, a sop to a gullible public. Insofar as it is seriously meant, it could also be seen as a search for interim solutions to cope with specific environmental problems like acid rain or nuclear waste disposal, until they can be 'solved' and growth can be resumed. Yet such explanations cannot suffice, for the problems involved have become too urgent. In West Germany in particular, acid rain, river and lake pollution and the perils of radiation from nuclear energy have become too dramatic ever to recede from the centre of politics. This is true of most other industrialised countries.

Most of the green-thinking prophets assume, with Kirkpatrick Sale, that some kind of 'techno-fix' solution will take precedence, at least in the short term, over more far-reaching changes. Sale acknowledges that human-scale development would in the best of circumstances, 'take several decades' since it calls for somewhat broader changes over time and the dislocation of powers that, despite being caught in recurrent double binds, retain considerable momentum. But he is sure the new age will come in the end:

It accords with some of the deepest instincts of the human animal, possibly encoded in our DNA, such as the drive for individual expresssion, for tribal and community sustenance, for harmony with the natural world of stars and trees and songbirds, for companionship and cooperation. It accords with the experience of by far the greater part of human history...(2)

Porritt, too, is optimistic. He is encouraged by the way green ideas have infiltrated, not only into established political parties, but peace movements, aid organisations like OXFAM, churches and other areas.

But how can this new world view break through? Porritt sees a chain of personal commitment, starting from humble beginnings:

People who are concerned about food and concerned about additives: that's bedrock stuff. People who are worried about insulating their houses, people who care more about recycling, taking advantage of bottle-banks and so on. And then you work through a whole succession of changes that involve a greater commitment as you go up the chain of personal responsibility. Right up to the point where you get people saying 'I will give a certain proportion of my income to other organisations or charities'—the lifestyle commitment which is asked of some people. Or people saying I want to change my job, I don't get any reward from this kind of stuff, I want to find alternative ways of generating income etc. You've got a whole continuum there. You then get the level of communities where, again, I think one is beginning to see a resurgence of a sense that the community matters to the individual who is living in it, and a readiness to take action to improve the environment—get rid of derelict sites, to making roads safe to school—a whole heap of tiny community initiatives. We've seen protests against a whole sequence of new road schemes—and there you begin to see very strongly the different attitudes at community level, where green thinking isn't called green, but it's absolutely rooted in the community.

Several green-thinking writers expect a political realignment, a move that will reflect increasing polarisation of society into 'two nations', in a deeper sense than the one Disraeli wrote about. James Robertson expects to see, on one side, the 'mainstream elements' of the main political parties, 'rooted in the institutions of late industrial society and its Business-as-Usual and hyper-expansionist tendencies'. On the other: the 'alternative, decentralising elements' in established parties and many Liberal and Green Party supporters and people of no political allegiance.

Several of the green prophets, like the prophets of old, see a collapse coming as a precursor of change. Like Robertson, Porritt predicts there will "inevitably be a fairly stark distinction between different approaches during a transition period, and if one envisages a gradual moving towards the green rather than a kind of sudden green revolution, then quite obviously there is going to be an absolutely critical point—I wouldn't like to put a date on it— but things according to our analysis are going to get tougher. The conventional ways of generating wealth, providing social services, looking after the environment, etc. are all going to become increasingly more difficult for governments."

As that happens two totally divergent developments will flow. The first will be those people who say 'it's not working, we've got to tighten up.' And that will be reflected both in governments' decisions and in individuals' decisions such as parents saying 'right, there's the system and we've got to make it work at all costs.' Totally opposite from that, flowing in a completely divergent direction, will be those people who say that as the system shrinks there's less and less in it for them and more and more incentive to find the alternatives. When I talk about this crunch time, it's a question of which of those two directions wins out. In my opinion the first one will have all the conventional power working with it, it will be backed by all the vested interests, by all the power blocks in our society, and will be accelerating a move to what I see as a quasi-totalitarian society in which participation is reduced to absolute minimum by a sequence of national and local legislative changes. The other one will have none of the conventional power with it but will have the vast welling up of human power, both in terms of disillusionment and in terms of that exciting discovery of what an alternative might mean. Now whether this power block is going to be sufficiently strong to overcome the first power block—I wouldn't like to conjecture.

So what can be done meanwhile? The prophets prescribe remedies for the state and for the individual. For the state, the favourite prescription is the Basic Income, in which the state consolidates all benefit payments, family and tax allowances, into a basic social wage, payable to everybody. The advantage as we have seen in chapter three, is that this would liberate people to lead more flexible and ultimately more useful lives. For the individual, change is feasible through personal transformation leading to community action.

The Basic Income is no panacea; it is not free from problems nor do all the green prophets accept it as desirable. We have seen that Guy Dauncey prefers new schemes for 'education for enterprise' and looks to local government to provide initiatives. He told us that he rejects the Basic Income because "it's a national scheme; it increases welfare dependency which is a horrific business. Also it's not viable: the level of finance will be very low, it will trap people into poverty; I believe in full employment, but the key to that is in work sharing, not Basic Income."

This strikes us as a partisan view. No amount of job-sharing and local government initiatives can bring in a new society, nor will teaching children to be little capitalists help them towards autonomy other than economic. The danger in Dauncey's vision is that the 'two nations', jobbed and unjobbed, of our declining industrial countries will become three: the conventionally employed, the unconventionally employed and a huge proletariat of the idle, unwanted unemployed.

Only Basic Income in some form, there are many varieties, can give people the autonomy and creativity they will need for breaking out of an outworn society into another. Jonathon Porritt acknowledged that even under such a scheme, "inconsistencies" will remain between private aspirations and ecological society, yet he accepts Basic Income as a bridge between societies.

How far must we decentralise? A Basic Income would be administered locally; and if the payments were made *as of right*, political interference could be minimised. However, there would need to be a central government and national as well as local accounting. Accordingly, Porritt speaks for the mainstream of modern green thinking, including Green parties, when he rejects extremes of decentralisation. There has to be a state:

> I don't have a philosophical objection to the notion of the state as the ringholder of the collective interests of all people in a country. I'm not an anarchic green or a fourth worlder; that approach to life is to me ludicrously nostalgic. It refers back to golden ages or idea about human communities that have little relevance and are singularly unhelpful in terms of getting across to people the utterly realistic alternatives that we've got. I'm increasingly critical of what I call the manic minisculists, people who think that life will suddenly be hunkydory if you do away with the nation state or the common market. I would see the state as exercising its present functions but in a more sensitive way: in terms of basic services like education, health, and income distribution. I mean the provision of resources to allow for equal access to a health service, and that means a real health service, not the thing we've got now—across the country. It all comes down to the distributive thing. If you allow all the social services— education, health and welfare—to be decentralised completely

and gave them fiscal, tax raising powers to allow for that decentralisation, then you would end up in my opinion with most regrettable regional disparities. I would always uphold the need for some distributive mechanism to ensure basic fairness across regions.

In their hearts, green thinkers don't place their hopes on politics at all. Their emphasis is on individual action. They see the way forwards as necessarily piecemeal—dependent on what people do for themselves. Schumacher expressed this strongly:

> It is the individual personal example that counts. The greatest 'doing' that is open to every one of us, now as always, is to foster and develop within oneself a genuine understanding of the situation which confronts us, and to build conviction, determination, and persuasiveness upon such understanding. Let us face it, to look at modern industry in the light of the Gospels is not the fashion of the day, and the diagnosis I have given here is not acceptable, at this point in time, to the great majority of our contemporaries. (3)

We put to Porrit the crunch question for the individual: can I live in this society and advocate a different one? He replied:

> It's not to do with asceticism and giving up everything, it's do do with the moderation and the responsibility of an individual consumer or a family unit. I don't see anything wrong in families having the accoutrements of conventional society like a television, washing machine and the rest of it; that's not the problem; the problem really is—what kind of attitudes do they try and encourage in their children in terms of how they're going to use their small amounts of pocket money, what kind of food they're going to buy and so forth. Are they setting a pattern which the children will see?

The best way to set a pattern is to act. People can easily initiate a community where nothing of the kind exists in their vicinity. Two or three neighbours are enough to make a start. They begin to pool knowledge of what is happening in the district, what is planned by individuals or authorities, what action could be taken to help good projects and hinder bad ones, what additional knowledge needs to be gathered, what contacts are available with local authorities, landowners or firms, which other local residents might help in particular ways. A group of that kind will grow naturally as more people are invited in for what they have to offer, or ask to join for what they might expect to gain.

That kind of group will be less structured than a parish council, though in the end, not necessarily smaller. It will set a pattern that runs counter to the closed nuclear family of industrial society. But the 'neighbourhood watch' that has become common in urban areas of Britain as a protection against burglars shows that informal joint action works, with agreeable side-effects. Many neighbourhood watch members find they have got to know the people in their street for the first time. Why stop at burglar-watching?

The informal community has great political potential. Whenever people gather local knowledge and do things for themselves, officials become less powerful and people have taken a first step to autonomy.

Notes:
(1) Illich, *Shadow Work*, page 22.
(2) Sale, *Human Scale*, page 37.
(3) Schumacher, *Good Work*, page 37.

Conclusion

We have been arguing throughout this book that the scientific paradigm (and here the word is appropriate) which comprises the fusion of Newtonian physics, Cartesian logic and Darwinian biology has become the dominant world view. Within that paradigm, the atom has been split, the surface of the moon walked upon, worn-out hearts have been replaced and people travel faster than sound. Images of these spectacular happenings have been watched by millions. Such events are labelled progress and they are so awe-inspiring that we tend to forget their consequences. But without moral human progress, scientific advance becomes increasingly dangerous. That has been said for a long time. Today, the urgency is new. We are poised to destroy the physical world by nuclear war or, failing that, by excess of 'economic development.' Even the privileged few who enjoy prosperity can no longer do so with an easy conscience. Affluence and technological progress which bring power and comfort to some, bring triviality, emptiness, boredom and hardship to many. Most of the world is underfed and under-housed, and poverty is creeping back into the heart of industrial societies, where a new proletariat of the jobless and the hopeless has been created.

Out of this crisis comes opportunity. Our materialist society shows signs of faltering, having ceased permanently to provide full employment. That fact alone dictates the need for a new one. New forms of society are consequently beginning to break through.

In this book we have sought the outlines of change. Our solution can be read as a blueprint (or greenprint) for a new society. But change begins most productively on the individual level. Can personal transformation lead to collective change? We have argued that the two are linked. Transformation of the individual and transformation of society are opposite sides of the same coin.

Wholeness and autonomy are the key ideas. They belong together; neither will be effective without the other. Wholeness without autonomy is inconceivable. And autonomy without wholeness amounts only to the narrow 'fulfilment' offered by consumer society—a 'happiness' that is enjoyed in privacy behind high hedges or inside motor cars.

Autonomy and wholeness are the best response to the apathetic fatalism that has locked our world onto a trajectory of doom. This fatalism leads to the notion that 'nothing' can stop the arms race, 'nobody' can halt the march of nuclear energy, or challenge the logic of multinationals, or stop the spoilation of the third world.

Only a whole and autonomous person can act, resist, walk away, build something new. Being whole, he or she can understand that the nuclear arms race is not maintained because of unthinking wickedness—but because the dynamic of a materialist, consumerist, expansionist and competitive society requires infinite growth. When every economy has to grow, available resources must shrink. If there is constant growth, each year's growth starts from a higher base: the process logically finishes when an island like Britain is covered over in asphalt. If happiness is freedom for the individual to prosper, some other individual, somewhere, must be impoverished.

As the new society breaks through, individual and political action will go together. A person, a family, a group, who have regained autonomy through *ownwork* and a simpler, richer, less consumerist lifestyle, will be relieved of fears for economic 'security', mortgages, savings and 'standard of living.' Anyone who wishes will therefore be free to vote for a political party offering a wider perspective on social change. Such parties scarcely exist today, except as marginal protest groups, because they have no chance of election. People are afraid, they lack the autonomy to vote for them.

We can measure the progress of the new society by looking at people, in the third world and the first, who have succeeded in decolonising themselves. They have become autonomous to a greater or lesser degree. That means: using their own resources, respecting their own environment, taking responsibility for their own work, food, leisure, culture, health and education. That does not imply isolation, or non-cooperation with other communities or with larger regional or national entities. It implies an end to exploiting in order to feel prosperous, and being exploited in order to feel secure. The green slogan 'act locally, think globally' can only become practical when a community has a minimum autonomy. There is no need to scrap specialist hospitals, schools or universities: there is a need to end dependence on such institutions.

The shift to wholistic thinking also means greater self-awareness, which is not the same as greater self-centredness. Islands of awareness are within ourselves. They exist in all of us, except those who have locked themselves into a consumerist, conformist and materialistic existence. This awareness of something better is also an awareness of something more real. That has been our theme. If we have helped anybody to discover more of that inner island, on which love is not an embarrassing word and where work and play are no longer disconnected, our writing will have been worthwhile.

Bibliography

Allen,Robert. *How to Save the World: Strategy for World Conservation* (Prentice-Hall, 1980).

Ash, Maurice. *New Renaissance: Essays in Search of Wholeness* (Green Books, 1987).

Bahro, Rudolf. *Building the Green Movement* (G.M.P., 1986).

Bahro, Rudolf. *From Red to Green* (Verso, 1984).

Ball, Colin & Mog. *Community Action and the School* (Penguin, 1973).

Bateson, Gregory. *Mind and Nature* (Wildwood House, 1979).

Berman, Morris. *The Re-enchantment of the World* (Cornell University Press, 1986).

Bohm, David. *Wholeness and the Implicate Order* (Ark, 1984).

Boston, Richard and others. *The Little Green Book* (The Green Alliance,1979).

Brown, Lester R. *Building a Sustainable Society* (W.W.Norton for World Watch Institute, New York, London, 1981).

Brown, Lester R. ed. *State of the World: Worldwatch Institute Report on Progress towards a Sustainable Society* (Norton. 1985 and 1986).

Callenbach, Ernest. *Ecotopia* (Banyan Tree Books, 1975).

Capra, Fritjof. *The Turning Point Science, Society and the Rising Culture* (Fontana, 1983).

Chardin, Teilhard de. *The Future of Man* (Fount, 1982).

Davies, Paul. *God and the New Physics* (Penguin, 1983).

Davies, Paul. *Superforce: The Search for a Grand Unified Theory of Nature* (Heinemann, 1984).

Devall, Bill & Sessions, George, *Deep Ecology*, Gibbs M. (Smith Inc., 1983, Salt Lake City).

Eckholm, Erik P. *Down to Earth: Environment and Human Needs* (Pluto Press, 1982).

Ekins, Paul. ed. *The Living Economy : A New Economics in the Making* (RKP, 1986).

Elgin, Duane. *Voluntary Simplicity* (William Morrow, New York 1981).

Ferguson, Marilyn. *The Aquarian Conspiracy* (Paladin Granada, 1982).

Fromm, Erich. *The Sane Society* (RKP, 1963).

Fromm, Erich. *The Anatomy of Human Destructiveness* (Holt, Rhinehart Winston, 1973).

Fromm, Erich, *To Have or To Be* (Abacus, 1979).

Grainger, Alan. *Desertification* (Earthscan 1982, reprinted 1986).

Goldsmith, Edward & Hildyard, Nicholas. *The Social and Environmental Effects of Large Dams* (Wadebridge Ecological Centre, 1984).

Goldsmith, Edward & Hildyard, Nicholas. eds. *Green Britain or Industrial Wasteland* (Polity Press 1986).

Gorz, Andre. *Paths to Paradise or the Liberation From Work* (Pluto, 1985)

Handy, Charles. *The Future of Work* (Basil Blackwell, 1984).

Hardin, Garrett. 'Tragedy of the Commons' *Science* (1968 no. 162) & *BioScience* (1974, no. 24).

Hawken, Paul. *The Next Economy* (Angus & Robertson, 1984).

Henderson, Hazel. *The Politics of the Solar Age: Alternatives to Economics* (Anchor books, 1981).

Illich, Ivan. *Deschooling Society* (Marion Boyars, 1972).

Illich, Ivan. *Shadow Work* (Marion Boyars, 1981).

Inglis, Brian. & West, Ruth. *The Alternative Health Guide* (Michael Joseph, 1983).

Inglis, Mary. & Kramer, Sandra. eds. *The New Economic Agenda* (Findhorn Press, 1985).

International Institute for Environmental Development. *World Resources 1986: An Assessment of the Resource Base That Supports the Global Economy* (Basic Books, New York. 1986).

Jaynes, Julian. *The Origin of Consciousness in the Breakdown of the Bicameral Mind* (Pelican, 1982).

Jung, C.G. *The Undiscovered Self* (RKP, 1958, 9th impression, 1982).

Kinsman, Francis. *The New Agenda* (Spencer Stuart, 1983).

Kumar, Satish. ed. *The Schumacher Lectures. Vols 1 & 11* (Abacus 1983, 1984).

Lane, John. *The Death and Resurrection of the Arts* (Green Alliance, 1982).

Laslett, Peter. *The World We Have Lost* (Methuen 1965, reprinted 1979).

Lovelock, Jim. *Gaia: A New Look at Life on Earth* (OUP, 1979).

McCormick, John. *Acid Earth: the global threat of acid pollution* (Earthscan, 1985).

McDonagh, Scan. *To Care For the Earth* (Cassell, 1986).

Martin, Vance & Inglis, Mary. eds. *Wilderness: The Way Ahead* (The Findhorn Press, 1984).

Maslow, Abraham H. *Towards a Psychology of Being* (2nd Edition. Van Nostrand Reinhold, 1968).

Mollison, Bill. *Permaculture Two: Practical Design for Town and Country in Permanent Agriculture* (Tagari, 1979).

Myers, Norman. ed. *The Gaia Atlas of Planet Management* (Pan Books, 1985)

Newbigin, Lesslie. *The Turn of The Tide* (BBC, 1986).

Newbigin, Lesslie. *Foolishness to the Greeks* (SPCK, 1986).

Osmond, John & Graham, Angela. *Alternatives: New Approaches to Health, Education, Energy, the Family and the Aquarian Age* (Thorsons, 1984).

Osmond, John. *Work in the Future: alternatives to unemployment* (Thorsons, 1986).

Papenek, Victor. *Design for the Real World: Human Ecology and Social Change* (Thames Hudson, 2nd edition. 1984).

Pepper, David. *The Roots of Modern Environmentalism* (Croom Helm, 1984).

Pietroni, Patrick. *Holistic living: a guide to self-care by a leading practitioner* (Dent, 1986).

Robertson, James. *The Sane Alternative: a choice of futures* (Revised edition, 1983) James Robertson, The Old Bakehouse, Cholsey, near Wallingford, Oxon. England.).

Robertson, James. *Future Work: jobs, self-employment and leisure after the Industrial Age* (Temple Smith-Gower, 1985).

Rowe, Dorothy. *Living with the Bomb: can we live without enemies?* (RKP, 1985).

Ruether, Rosemary Radford. *New Woman New Earth: Sexist Ideologies & Human Liberation* (The Seebury Press, 1975).

Russell, Peter. *The Awakening Earth; The Global Brain* (Ark, 1982, reprinted 1985).

Sale, Kirkpatrick, *Human Scale* (Secker & Warburg, 1980).

Sale, Kirkpatrick. *Dwellers in the Land; The Bioregional Vision* (Sierra Club, San Francisco, 1985).

Schumacher, Diana and others. *Energy: Crisis or Opportunity? An Introduction to Energy States* (Macmillan, 1985).

Schumacher, E.F. *Small is Beautiful: A Study of Economics as if People Mattered* (Abacus, 1974).

Schumacher, E.F. *A Guide for the Perplexed* (Abacus, 1978).

Schumacher, E.F. *Good Work* (Abacus, 1980).

Seymour, John, *The Forgotten Arts* (Dorling Kindersley/The National Trust, 1984).

Sheldrake, Rupert. *A New Science of life; The Hypothesis of Formative Causation* (Paladin, 1983 reprinted 1984).

Simon, Brian & Taylor, William. *Education in the Eighties: The Central Issues* (Batsford, 1981).

Simon, Julian & Kahn, Herman. eds. *The Resourceful Earth: A Response to Global 2000* (Basil Blackwell, 1984).

Timberlake, Lloyd. *Africa in Crisis: The Causes, The Cures of Environmental Bankruptcy* (Earthscan, 1985).

Tobias, Michael. ed. *Deep Ecology* (Avant Books, 1984).

Trevelyan, George. *A Vision of the Aquarian Age: The Emerging Spiritual World View* (Coventure.1984).

Toogood, Philip. *The Head's Tale* (Dialogue Publications, 1984).

Van de Weyer, Robert. *Wickwyn: A Vision of the Future* (SPCK, 1986).

Waller, Robert. *The Agricultural Balance Sheet* (The Green Alliance, 1982).

Ward, Keith. *The Turn of the Tide: Christian Belief in Britain Today* (BBC, 1986).

Woodward, Lawrence, *The Alternative View: Organic farming* (Elm Farm Research Centre, 1984).

Wookey, Barry. *Rushall: the Story of an Organic Farm,* (Basil Blackwell, 1987)

Worster, Donald. *Nature's Economy* (CUP, 1985).

Zukov, Gary. *The Dancing Wu-Li Masters:An Overview of the New Physics* (Flamingo, 1984).

Index

Agriculture, 149-167
Africa, 8, 93, 101
Art, 63-67
  and women, 91
Bahro, Rudolf, 11, 92, 237
Basic Income, 27, 42-45, 50,
  261, 262
Berman, Morris, 144
Bio-regions, 20, 139-143
Bohm, David, 245
Bookchin, Murray, 134
Browne, Lester R.
  & Wolfe, Edward C., 24
Capra, Fritjof, 126, 129, 153,
  156, 175, 178, 182, 240
Chardin, Teillard de, 191, 248
Chernobyl, *Intro*, 113, 114, 115,
  129
Chipko Movement, 102-3
Communities, 22, 80-84
  Crabapple, 80-82
  Lower Shaw Farm, 82-84
  Pleck Community Assn., 73
  Lightmoor, 62-63,
  health care, 181-183
  colleges, 224
Computers, 74, 119-121
Co-operatives, 76-78
Dauncey, Guy, 22, 23, 61, 73,
  216, 246-7, 261
Davies, Paul, 243-4
Elgin, Duane, 6
Easterhouse, 71-73, 74-75
Ecologist, The, 113, 115, 166
  Blueprint for Survival, 135
Ecology, 125-145
Economics, New, 33-51
Economy, grassroots, 72, 73-74,
  91, 102

Education, 213-231
  de-schoolers, 218-220
  for enterprise, 215-218
  Fiveways Primary School, 229-230
  Manifesto, 225-227
  The Small School, 225-226
  schools in Denmark, 231
  White Lion Free School, 227-
  229
Energy, 112-119
  in agriculture, 153-155
  conservation, 116-119
  nuclear, 113-116
Ferguson, Marylyn, 195, 240
Fromm, Erich, 13, 25, 29, 34,
  192, 193, 236
Gaia,
  hypothesis, 135-137
  myth, 137, 248
Goldsmith, Edward, 66, 101
Gortz, Andre, 60
Greens, 135, 201
  British, 254-255
  money, 45-48
  polititians, 255-257
  women, 198-203
Green Revolution, 9, 89, 150
  and women, 206
Handy, Charles:
  Basic Income, 42
  hours of work, 58
  education, 214-215
Hardin, Garrett, 133-134
Health, 20, 28, 171-185
Henderson, Hazel, 36, 39
Illich, Ivan, 41, 254
  on development, 91-92
  on education, 218-219
  shadow work, 59

Jaynes, Julian, 196-197

Kinsman, Francis, 198-199, 209

Lasslett, Peter, 55-56

LETS, (Local Exchange Trading System) 46-47

Lovelock, James, 136, 248

McRobie, George, 110-111

McDonagh, Sean, 247-248

Maxneef, Manfred, 39, 92, 95

Mollison, Bill, 165

Naess, Arne, 126, 129, 130, 131, 132, 167

Newbiggin, Leslie, 4, 242, 244

Organic farming, 156-164

Papenek, Victor, 37

Pietroni, Dr. Patrick, 179, 185

Pepper, David, 14, 135

Permaculture, 22, 164-167

Porritt, Jonathan, *Intro,* 93, 95, 101, 197-8, 255-6, 258-263

Rowe, Dorothy, 4

Robertson, James, 13, 26, 28
   on Basic Income, 43, 57, 182, 260

Russell, Peter, 248

Sale, Kirkpatrick, 257-258

Schumacher, Fritz, *Intro,* 24, 37-38
   on work, 57, 90-91
   on technology, 109-110
   on education, 220-223, 236
   heirarchy of being, 238-240, 263

Seymour, John, 67

Technology, appropriate, 27, 37 109 -121

Third World
   women in, 204-206
   development, 89-105

Timberlake, Lloyd, 94

Waller, Robert, 152

Ward, Keith, 242-243, 244-245

Weyer, Robert Van de, 7

Women, 13, 43, 189-209

Wookey, Barry, 160-162

Worster, Donald, 128, 130, 132-133